Faith

Great Christian Truths

The Faith

Great Christian Truths

PETER MASTERS

Wakeman Trust, London

THE FAITH
© Peter Masters 2006

THE WAKEMAN TRUST
(Wakeman Trust is a UK Registered Charity)

UK Registered Office
38 Walcot Square
London SE11 4TZ

US Office
300 Artino Drive
Oberlin, OH 44074-1263
Website: www.wakemantrust.org

ISBN   1 870855 54 X
ISBN-13 978 1 870855 54 9

Cover design by Andrew Owen

Printed by Stephens & George, Merthyr Tydfil, UK

Contents

1

The Mysterious Nature of a Soul

Man has a soul of vast desires
And burns within with restless fires.

W E BEGIN this overview of great Christian truths with a look at the *creature* rather than the Creator, because, while God is obviously infinitely greater and more glorious, man was created to be unique on Earth, possessing an eternal soul with remarkable properties. Man is the zenith, the very highest point, of God's creative activity. There can be no greater tragedy, and no greater darkness, than men and women who live through life unaware of their status and capacities in God's plan and purpose. A clear knowledge of the human constitution provides an essential foundation for understanding life, and also spurs people to seek after the eternal God.

If secular society retained even the smallest realisation of the unique nature of man there would be no devaluing of people to the level of higher animals, no scrapping of moral values, and far less indifference to the Creator.

The authoritative word about the soul is to be found in *Genesis 2.7* – 'And the Lord God formed man of the dust of the ground, and breathed into his nostrils the breath of life; and man became a living soul.' Here the distinctive nature of human beings is asserted, the body being formed from pre-existing matter, but the soul being breathed directly into the body by the power of God. Animals by contrast are very firmly said to have been brought forth from the Earth only.[1] Furthermore, man is exclusively said to be made 'in the image of God', and so he is pronounced superior to all animals.[2]

Man, therefore, consists of two 'elements', a body and a soul, the one being material and mortal, and the other immaterial and immortal.[3] The soul is the *real* person, the distinctive identity or personality. The Bible everywhere distinguishes between soul and body, sometimes portraying the body as a garment for the soul, or as the tent or house in which the soul lives. The body will eventually be laid aside at death, but the soul will live on. The body will be reduced to dust, but the soul will retain eternally its consciousness and activity,[4] to be either with God in Heaven or banished from his presence.[5]

In the Bible the soul is the organ of rational thought, and the seat of a person's emotions and will. Because the soul is not material, you cannot see it by dissecting the body or the brain, although it uses the brain. Secularists sneer at the idea of the soul, claiming that all human thought and activity is entirely produced by chemical processes in the brain. They say that any notion of a soul is an invention of ancient times when people did not know about the role of brain cells. However, it has always been understood that the brain is the means by which the soul functions, the 'operations room' of the soul, because even the ancients knew that if someone received a really

---

1   *Genesis 1.24; 2.19*
2   *Genesis 1.26-28*
3   *Matthew 10.28; 16.26; 1 Corinthians 15.53; 2 Corinthians 5.4*
4   *2 Corinthians 5.1-8; Genesis 2.7; Genesis 3.19; Ecclesiastes 12.7*
5   *Matthew 25.21, 34, 46; 2 Thessalonians 1.7-10; 2 Timothy 4.8*

hard crack on the head he would be concussed, becoming confused at the least, and possibly never quite the same again. They realised that the soul required the brain in order to relate to the material world.

The soul, however, is more than the brain, embracing as we have already noted the mind, will and emotions, along with the personality and 'spirit'; this last is a person's potential for spiritual activity. The soul uses the brain just as a musician uses an instrument to make music. This is why some features of personality are inherited, because the brain as an instrument resembles that of the parents. However, according to Scripture, there is an independent personality – a soul – behind the brain, and no two people are ever the same, nor do they react in exactly the same way in any situation.[6] The secularist says there is no independent person or mind resident in one's head, only a complex computer, but the Bible holds up the human soul as unique in the animal kingdom, and accountable to its Creator.

The start of one's life is the beginning of the history of an eternal, never-dying soul, there being no prior existence for the soul. Because God is described as the 'Father of spirits',[7] we understand that the soul is created directly by him at the outset of life. Our bodies, therefore, are derived from our earthly parents, but our souls from God.

The soul is not in any way an extension of God, or made of the divine essence, for it is a created thing. A person's soul or spirit is distinguished from that of an angel's because it has been designed to be united with a body, whereas angels are spirits created to function without bodies.

What exactly can the soul do? The range of abilities given to every human soul is astonishing, and for this reason anyone who does not

---

6   *Psalm 139.14-16* breathes the individuality of God's fashioning of people.
7   *Hebrews 12.9*

understand and appreciate his soul has missed the whole point of his existence. In these next pages we list the abilities or departments or faculties of the soul, five in all.

Five Faculties of the Soul

1 The first faculty of the soul is the *mind* or the *reason,* which enables people to know, think and imagine; to understand moral precepts; to weigh the pros and cons of any situation; and to plan. Here is wisdom unique to the human race.[8]

2 The second faculty of the soul is the *will,* by which all choices are exercised and implemented and a person determines to act in any given way. The will is the 'executive arm' of the soul.[9]

3 The third faculty of the soul is the emotional part, also called the *affections* or the feelings. Many Christian writers include this faculty with the mind, but we give it a separate heading in line with the three faculties of the soul mentioned in *Proverbs 3.5-6,* namely the *heart* (emotions), the *understanding* (mind), and the *ways* (will). The emotions respond to or endorse whatever is considered by the mind, and also to situations and events, and include a person's tastes and desires. The capacity for happiness, delight, sorrow, compassion, and love is frequently mentioned in Scripture.[10]

The emotions should ideally be governed by the mind, but they can charge off on their own, rather as a drunken or drugged person may act without rational control. Since the Fall of man (described in chapter 5), the affections are corrupted and inclined to seek

---

8 *Proverbs 3.5; Matthew 22.37; Romans 7.25; Philippians 2.5; 2 Timothy 1.7*
9 *1 Corinthians 7.37; 2 Corinthians 8.3, 12; Philippians 2.13*
10 Eg: the NT 'bowels' texts where the spleen as an organ is a figure of deep feelings of tender love, mercy, compassion, etc. *Philippians 2.1; Colossians 3.12; Philemon v 7; 1 John 3.17.* See also *Deuteronomy 33.29; Psalm 128.1-2; Psalm 144.15.*

satisfaction in bodily desires and lusts, and selfish ends.[11]

To summarise so far, the powers or faculties of the soul are the mind, the will, and the emotions, but there are two further faculties of vital importance. None of the three aspects of the soul just reviewed are seen in animals except in a very simple, limited way, and tied to the animal's instincts. Having no soul, animals have no power to reason, no freedom of choice and no refinement of feeling. Any limited appearance of these abilities is related to an animal's instinctual need of provision and survival. Rudimentary affection or loyalty, for example, are merely expressions of – 'the ox knoweth his owner, and the ass his master's crib.'

4 The fourth faculty of the soul shines a light over the first three because it is the voice of God's law in the soul, the *conscience*, a resident magistrate within. Solomon called it the lamp of the Lord searching all the inward parts.[12] The *conscience* works in the mind to stir moral awareness and to accuse or excuse all that is done.[13] The mind (the first faculty we have listed) is already stamped with the moral law of God, having an intuition to know right and wrong, and the conscience stands alongside the mind, much as police and magistrates monitor the behaviour of society. Speaking to the mind (and through the mind to the emotions) the conscience causes either pain or pleasure as it reacts to the thoughts and schemes of the mind, and the actions of the will. This twofold knowledge of God's standards is most carefully set out by Paul, who says (first) that people show the law written in their hearts, then (secondly) conscience also bears witness, giving judgement on their deeds.[13]

The conscience may be trampled down and rendered insensible by human determination to sin. It is not therefore infallible, and if wilfully re-programmed will become a perverted and deceiving

---

11 *Ephesians 2.3; 1 Peter 2.11*
12 *Proverbs 20.27*
13 *Romans 2.14-15*

conscience.[14] However, it is indestructible and will always react righteously to some degree even in the most depraved person, because God's standards can never be entirely eradicated.[15] Needless to say a conscience is not seen in animals.

5 The fifth power or faculty of the soul should really be given first place because it stands high above the others, enabling people to fulfil the glorious purpose of their creation – that of interacting with their God. It is the faculty of spiritual communion, the ability to speak to the Lord in praise and in prayer. This power of the soul is referred to in the Bible by the word *spirit.* The terms soul and spirit are largely interchangeable in the New Testament,[16] both of them describing the soul, but each term having a distinctive purpose. The term *soul* refers to the whole soul (all its faculties) whereas the term *spirit* speaks specifically of the power of the soul to engage in spiritual participation with God.

Is it right to say that the spirit is dead in people who have no walk with God, and do not communicate with him? In one sense it is,[17] but because people are responsible for their sin we equally say that their spirits are inactive. Just as it may be said of someone that he has a brain and will not use it, so it may be said that he has a soul but will not pray.

Equipped with a soul, man is seen to be created in the image and likeness of God.[18] Because God has no body, man can only resemble God in terms of his soul and all its capabilities, namely the power of reason, the power of decision, sophisticated emotions, moral consciousness, and the potential for spiritual interaction. By our souls we reflect our Creator, however faintly.

---

14 *1 Timothy 4.2; Hebrews 9.14*

15 *John 8.9*

16 In two texts – *1 Thessalonians 5.23* and *Hebrews 4.12* – they are mentioned together ('spirit and soul', and 'soul and spirit').

17 *Ephesians 2.1*

18 *Genesis 1.26-27*

How Much Does Man Still Reflect God?

By man's disobedience and fall in the Garden of Eden (examined in chapter 5), and through the corruption of his nature, the image of God in him has been greatly spoiled, yet he continues to bear surviving features of his created glory. One great writer put it in these words: 'The soul's *essence* is preserved, though it has been robbed of its heavenly adornments.' Only Jesus Christ the Lord perfectly reflected on Earth the glory of God,[19] and converted people are so changed that they begin to improve as image-bearers, and eventually enter Heaven instantly made perfect by divine power.[20]

Bearing in mind the powers or faculties of the soul, we know that every person, converted or unconverted, continues to be in the image of God, however imperfectly, in the following ten ways: –

(1) He or she is a personal being with individual conscious existence and power of action.

(2) He possesses the mental power to think about all things in the world around him. He has, in other words, the gift of reason; the thinking, reflecting, planning faculty.

(3) He possesses that power of choice between alternatives, which marks him out as a free agent (although now so often dominated by the earthly and physical desires which most please him). He is not subject to mere animal instincts, but can choose between them.

(4) He possesses a moral consciousness or awareness (the remains of his original holy nature) augmented by a conscience which calls out, 'I ought to do this,' or, 'I ought not'.

(5) He possesses, despite the Fall, traces and remains of moral virtues, together with some ability to regulate his outward behaviour in life. For this reason he has no excuse for sin. He

---

19 *Colossians 1.15; 2 Corinthians 4.4*
20 *Romans 8.29; 2 Corinthians 3.18*

has lost, however, his natural and willing obedience to all God's law.

(6) He possesses perpetual existence, or immortality, in his soul, this immortality being supplied and sustained by God. Eternal *existence* is not the same as eternal *life,* however, because at the time of physical death the soul may be sentenced to exist eternally in a state of spiritual death. In other words it may be ever-existent in hell.

(7) He possesses also, despite the Fall, a measure of dominion over other creatures, a glory given to him in Eden as a reflection of God's dominion. So he reflects God by possessing (above other creatures) unique attributes and dignity.

(8) He still possesses since the Fall a remaining *natural,* instinctual awareness of God, along with an ability to see God's power and Godhead in the works of creation.

(9) He still possesses since the Fall a considerable measure of the inclination to *love* and *relate to* fellow-creatures in a feelingful way, for he continues to be, like God, a 'relational' being. He desires love and relationships, and, uniquely among creatures, he is capable of language. Though hostility has become deeply embedded in his nature through the Fall, these powerful indications remain of his being created in God's likeness.

(10) He still possesses, after the Fall, the capacity for intelligent happiness and delight. Unlike animals, his intelligence is a creative, inventive intelligence, able to design and carry out innovations of great complexity and beauty. However, man has lost (through sin) the intense happiness and glory of finding his greatest delight in God.

As we consider these things, do we appreciate the uniqueness of our human nature, and the privilege of being image-bearers of the Creator? Do we realise our potential for spiritual communion with God, which is the ultimate purpose of life? Are we aware that we must one day give account to God for how we have stewarded our most priceless possession – the soul? Surely the greatest responsibility in life is to seek and find the Lord, to learn of him and serve him, and so to fulfil the profound words of an historic catechism – 'The chief end of man is to glorify God and to enjoy him for ever.'

How did mankind fall from favour and communion with God? This tragic event will be described in this book shortly, but first we review the greatest possible theme for the human mind – the nature and attributes of God himself.

CAN mortals understand or find
The perfect, uncreated Mind?
And can the greatest human thought
Measure and search God's nature out?

'Tis high as Heaven, and deep as well;
What can mere mortals know or tell?
His glory spreads beyond the sky
And all the starry worlds on high.

Isaac Watts

2

God's Exclusive Attributes

'I am God, and there is none else; I am God,
and there is none like me' *(Isaiah 46.9)*.

DOWN THE CENTURIES of time many people have been
moved to value and seek God on hearing about his glorious nature and qualities – his attributes. Christians also
have found a major deepening of their spiritual lives has come from
a greater realisation of the majesty and wonder of their God. How
much do we know about our Creator, his characteristics and his
ways?

God's attributes are his qualities or perfections expressed as far as
it is possible to do in words. His attributes describe him, and in a
sense they *are* him. They set out his nature as far as human minds
can grasp it. These attributes should not be thought of as separate
departments of God, as though he consisted of parts connected
together. All God's attributes are really one, being fused together

and extending through his infinite being. They are only mentioned individually in the Bible as a means of helping finite human minds to understand the divine glory. It may be said that God does not *have* these glorious qualities, he *is* these qualities.

Some of the divine attributes are *exclusive to God*, not being seen at all in created beings, whether angels or people. These exclusive, unique attributes are the following. God consists of divine spiritual essence and is self-existent (or self-energising). He is infinite, eternal, immense, omnipresent and unchangeable. (These are technically called the *incommunicable* attributes because God does not communicate or share them.) The greatest mystery of all, but vital for appreciating God, is that he is one God in three persons, all equally God and in perfect harmony.

Other attributes of God are (in different degrees) reflected in angels and people. These are the following: power, knowledge, wisdom, truthfulness, faithfulness, holiness, justice, goodness and love. (These are called *communicable* attributes.)

In this chapter we shall describe the six mighty attributes or qualities of God that are exclusive to himself, followed in the next two chapters by nine attributes that are reflected in angels and human beings.

1. God is Divine Spirit

The first quality or attribute exclusive to God is that he is *divine spirit*, his 'essence' being glorious beyond human imagination, incomprehensible and invisible to us.[1] Angelic spirits do not share the essence of God, nor do human souls. Though the ransomed souls in Heaven see Christ in his glorified body and observe his character and ways, they will never be able to see his divine nature or being.[2]

---

1   *John 4.24; Deuteronomy 4.15-16*
2   *1 Timothy 1.17; 1 Timothy 6.16; Exodus 33.20*

God's *glory* will surely be perceived in Heaven by the senses, but not his being.[3]

The spiritual 'substance' or 'essence' of God requires no body, and has no bodily passions, or passions stimulated by bodily drives and needs. God certainly does know love, anger, desire, and grief, but in a most perfect and holy form. He has no feelings like our 'lower' feelings generated from the body, such as hunger for food or care or other *bodily* gratification, whether good or bad. Obviously he has no unholy feelings such as greed, jealousy, lust, base hatred and hostility.

Because God is divine spirit and beyond our grasp and sight there is no way we can discover him or know his will by our power of reason. God's infinite intelligence and power may certainly be seen in the created universe,[4] but for man to know more, God must reveal himself to the human race, which he has done in his inspired Word, without which all speculation about him is vain.[5]

Because God is divine spirit he cannot be illustrated by human art. It would be an insult to his divine attributes to attempt to do so (as we learn from the second commandment), because the greatest and most imaginative art will fall far short of his glory, failing to depict infinite values, and thereby reducing his attributes to a human level. How can that which is finite ever begin to illustrate or represent the infinite? The best we can do is to employ words, and these must be the words that God uses to describe himself.[6]

The Reformers were very firm on this point, insisting that the second commandment demanded that likenesses or images of God should (firstly) not be made, nor (secondly) worshipped, the first prohibition including their use for instruction or pleasure.

Because he is the divine spirit, infinitely glorious, God cannot

---

3   *Exodus 33.22-23*
4   *Romans 1.19-21; Psalm 19.1-3*
5   *Hebrews 1.1-2; 2 Peter 1.19; Psalm 145.18*
6   *Exodus 20.4; Isaiah 40.12, 18, 25; John 4.24; Philippians 3.3*

be pleased or entertained by human offerings, ceremonies, music, incense, or similar things. Singing and musical accompaniment are merely *vehicles* and *helps* in worship, but the real worship is *words* projected to God from sincere hearts. In Old Testament times ceremonies such as sacrifices were intended to prefigure and teach about a coming Saviour, not to delight God's senses.[7] The Lord may only be worshipped 'in spirit and in truth',[8] which means by faith, and in line with the kind of worship laid down in the Bible.

2. God is Self-Existent

The second attribute exclusive to God is his *self-existence*. He is 'the living God',[9] who, in speaking to Moses, gave himself a five-word name – 'I AM THAT I AM',[10] showing that he is the everlasting present tense and the supreme source of all life, who alone possesses the power of existence. We derive life from him, and without his support we would disintegrate, but God's life is from himself. He is therefore *self-existent*, needing no other power either to bring him into existence, or to feed and sustain him. He needs no help from anywhere, and nothing could possibly add to him.[11] Not one part of God is derived from outside himself.

As the source of all other life, God created angels, the universe, and mankind. He was never created and can never be destroyed. No wonder Christ by his inherent power of life was able to rise from the dead! By using the formal name 'I AM' God showed that he was not an impersonal force, but a living, conscious, knowable God, having an identity. He also announced himself to be the exclusive God, by contrast with the numerous idols of human invention. (Being one

---

7   *1 Samuel 15.22; Psalm 40.6-8; Psalm 51.16; Proverbs 21.3; Micah 6.6-8;*
    Matthew 9.13; Hebrews 10.5-9
8   *John 4.24*
9   *John 5.26; Jeremiah 10.10*
10 *Exodus 3.14*
11 *Acts 17.25*

God does not contradict his triune being, described in chapter 10.)

The uniqueness of God's nature or essence is also brought out by the name – 'I AM' – for it elevates him above all created things. He does not enter into composition with them so that they become divine and share his being. There is no similarity of essence between God and created matter, because he ever remains distinct from and transcendent over all that he has made.

Satan and demons, being fallen angels, do not possess the power of existence or life in themselves, and will therefore fall at God's sentence of condemnation along with all people, however powerful, who make themselves enemies of their Creator and Sustainer.[12]

This second attribute of God – that he is the sole, self-existing fountain of all life and being – is the essential foundation for reverence and trust. It is the basis of God's right to carry out his will in the created universe, to demand our allegiance, and to call us to account in the last great day. His divine being must be acknowledged, and he must be held in awe.

3. God is Infinite

The third attribute exclusive to God is his *infinity*. All his attributes are limitless in their scope and perfection, and beyond measurement.[13] His power, knowledge, wisdom and love, for example, are so great that they extend without limit beyond all possible comprehension, and can never be exhausted. We now show separately God's infinity in relation to time and space.

4. God is Eternal

The fourth attribute exclusive to God applies infinity to *time*. God is *eternal*. He is not only everlasting by the measurement of time, but

---

12 *Revelation 20.10-15*
13 *Romans 11.33; 1 Kings 8.27*

he is above and outside time, or timeless, having no beginning and no end.[14]

God is therefore of infinite age, for he always has been, and this is equally true of the Father, the Son and the Holy Spirit, all being equally God, in one Godhead. God cannot age, decline, or decay, nor can there be any growth or development in him, because if this occurred he would not be eternally perfect, having needed to develop his qualities.

Time has been defined as a succession of moments existing one at a time. The previous moment no longer exists; the next moment does not yet exist. Men and angels live within this narrow moving spectrum of experience, but God is far above this, seeing all history, past, present and future, at the same time. Yet by his infinite intelligence he distinguishes every moment from the next, and is able to act towards mankind and identify with us, as though he were living in time alongside us.[15]

Time is a measure of duration designed for created beings and things, all of which are susceptible to age and change. Angels (with the exception of those that fell with Satan) are sustained by God so that they cannot age or taste death, but, like human beings they live within a framework of time. Apart from what they have been taught by God, they do not know what will happen in the future, but keenly watch the unfolding work of redemption on Earth.[16] They are still learning, because they are subject to time and development.

Ransomed people also, when in Heaven, will continue to live within a framework of time, but it will be time that will last for ever. They will not see all the eternal history of bliss at a glance, as God sees it, and why should they want to? Times of awe, insight, discovery, happiness and love will be tasted with rapture hour by hour.

---

14 *Deuteronomy 33.27; Psalm 29.10; Psalm 45.6; Psalm 48.14; Psalm 90.2;*
    Psalm 102.27; Isaiah 40.28; Isaiah 57.15; 1 Timothy 1.17
15 *Exodus 32.9-10; 1 Samuel 15.11*
16 *Ephesians 3.10; 1 Peter 1.12*

Only the infinite, sovereign, transcendent God is outside time.[17]

Just as God is eternal, so are his will, his Word, and his promises, none of which will ever fail or die. Why do people trust in human leaders, human technology, human promises, and human learning, all of which fail frequently, and pass with time? Why are we so prone to forget the eternal being of our God?

5. God is Immeasurably Immense and Present Everywhere

Our fifth attribute or perfection exclusive to God applies infinity to *space,* for God is infinitely *immense.* The divine essence has no boundaries or limits; God is everywhere, stretching endlessly beyond the vastness of space.[18]

God's immensity includes the fact that he is present everywhere, or omnipresent, his power being in every particle and space in creation. It has been said that he is present in every drop of blood in the body, and in the tiniest unit of substance. This does not mean that all things contain the divine essence of God, because the things that God creates do not become divine. We have already observed that he is transcendent over his creation, meaning he is apart from it, and yet his presence permeates all things. Created things, including angels and men, are not composed of the being of God, but all things, however tiny, are suspended in his constant presence, view, and power.

God is not to be compared with the sun, or with a lighthouse, or a radio transmitter, which all remain in their place while their influence reaches other places. God does not merely influence

---

17 Thus statements such as *Revelation 10.6* to the effect that time will end, refer to the present time or era, and not the abolition of the medium of time within which we were created. The new heavens and earth constitute a restoration of paradise, not a removal of the entire structure of human existence.

18 *1 Kings 8.27; Psalm 139.6-12; Isaiah 66.1; Jeremiah 23.23-24; Acts 17.24*

everywhere, his presence *is* everywhere. It is difficult for finite minds to grasp the immensity of God, because he is infinitely greater than our utmost comprehension, and his thoughts and ways far, far higher than ours.[19]

Angels and men cannot be present in more than one place at the same time, but God is everywhere at the same time. The only way of sensing and appreciating God's presence is to see him in Scripture, by believing his description of himself and his purposes.

Christians are strengthened in several areas of belief when they reflect on God's omnipresence:

(i) They become assured that he sees all things.

(ii) They are stirred to worship a God of towering majesty, and to honour him worthily for who he is.

(iii) They have wholesome fear promoted in their hearts, and their trust is strengthened, for who could not trust a God so mighty and immense as to swallow up creation a million times, and at the same time be so close to us that he sustains every particle in the body?

6. God is Unchangeable

The sixth attribute exclusive to God is *unchangeability*. He can neither change nor be changed by any outside force. He is immutable,[20] or to put it another way, he is both constant and consistent. We observe once again that if this were not so, God would not be perfect, because change could only make an utterly perfect God less perfect, or *vice versa*, and God needs no revision or modification.

God must be unchangeable to be faithful to all his attributes, upholding them all, because if any fell, he would not continue to be wholly God. He cannot deny his nature. Therefore his eternal qualities and perfections have never altered, and will never do so in the future.

19 *Isaiah 55.8-9*
20 *1 Samuel 15.29; Malachi 3.6; Romans 1.23; Hebrews 13.8; James 1.17*

The unchangeableness of God, however, does not mean that he is static or immobile, for he is always active, exercising his attributes and bringing to pass his plans and purposes for mankind and the universe. For example, we see him in the records of the Bible constantly observing and responding to sin, either to punish evil or to forgive those who repent. He constantly listens to prayers and responds, changing situations, or equipping people to endure them.

Scripture sometimes portrays God as repenting, implying that he changes his mind, but this expression is used to describe how God changes his way of dealing with people in response to their behaviour, blessing faithfulness, or taking benefits away from the faithless.[21] In other words, God 'repents' in the sense that he changes his treatment of people in line with his promises or warnings to them. There will never be any change in the standards that God follows, nor in his purposes, or promises. His kingdom will stand for ever and his mercy will never fade. Living as we do in a world of constant change and decay, with the debris of failure, broken promises and disappointments strewn everywhere, who would not trust a God who is the Rock of Ages, unchanging, unfailing and infinitely reliable?

* * *

These six sublime attributes that are exclusive to God should be treasured in the minds of believers, because a deep realisation of God's majesty and glory is the foundation of their love, and loyalty and worship.[22] A perpetual appreciation of God's perfections increases trust and stirs gratitude for amazing grace. Thinking of them causes human pride to retreat and humility to flourish, bringing about willing submission to such a God.

21 *Genesis 6.2-7; Jonah 3.3-10*
22 *Revelation 5.13*

3

The Reflected Attributes of God
Power – Knowledge – Wisdom – Truth

'O the depth of the riches both of the wisdom and knowledge of God!
how unsearchable are his judgments, and his ways past finding out!'
(Romans 11.33)

I N SOME WAYS we can appreciate the perfections of Almighty
God even more by looking at the attributes that he has
imparted in a small degree to us as image-bearers. We can only
grasp God's infinity and eternity at an intellectual level, but we have
personal experience of the reflected or 'communicable' attributes.
Because, for example, we have a certain amount of power ourselves,
we can better appreciate the nature of God's overwhelming power.
It is true that the greatest human power is a poor illustration of the
infinite power of God, but by drawing contrasts as we shall now do,
our understanding is stimulated. (All these reflected attributes are,
in the case of God, self-generated, infinite, eternal, immense, and
unchangeable. In our case they are none of these things.)

The Power of God

God's mighty power, the first in our list of reflected qualities, is distinctive because it is a true *creating* power, only he being able to create out of nothing, and to destroy.[1] Human beings are extremely creative, exercising originality not seen in animals, but our creativity must use pre-existing materials, and when we 'destroy' we merely change something in form, as when fire turns things to ash, or drives gases into the air. God's power is also far, far beyond ours in that he is able to perform creative acts on both a massive and a microscopic scale. Our mediocre power must be exercised within a very limited range of possibilities.

God's power is altogether above ours because it is an *inexhaustible, self-sustaining* power costing him no toil, exertion or pain, whereas any action that we take requires energy and bodily nourishment. Just as a battery runs down we age and tire, being unable to sustain ourselves let alone impart vigour to others. But the unfading, perpetual power of God upholds and sustains the universe with ease.

Unlike us God needs no help or assistance to do anything, and so his power is truly *independent and free*. He is not like the moon which must derive light from the sun. He is not in debt to anyone, owes no favours, and his power is not hampered or compromised by any situation such as the limitations of a civil service, or the need to ingratiate an electorate. He is above all other power, originates all other power, and can take away all other power when he pleases.

God's power is *absolute,* meaning that he can do anything his holy, infinitely wise mind decides. His power is infinitely great, so that none can overwhelm or defeat him, nor can he be resisted if he acts against anyone. His power is also irresistible in the salvation of men and women. We have a small measure of power but we cannot do everything we choose, nor can we always do things the moment we

---

1 *Romans 1.20*

choose to do them. We usually need help, and can only act when circumstances allow, whereas God's absolute and invincible power is always exercised at the exact moment he determines.

God's power is also a *spectacular* power. When he makes bare his arm to do great things in the universe, the result may be breathtaking in beauty or terrifying in devastation. He does astounding things in nature, and also in the lives of people when he forgives and re-makes them in salvation.

Yet God's power is a *controlled* power, for he frequently holds it back to express his mercy, delaying judgement for millions in order to save souls still unborn. Human power is so often uncontrolled, driven by a spirit of recklessness, selfishness, hatred or vengeance, even to the point of self-destruction, but God's power is never out of his control. We may think of the intricate 'power' of microsurgery, but nothing can be compared with the gentle power of God in the renewing of believers, and the exercise of his divine patience.

God is supreme and above all limitations except that his power is a *holy* power, and he will never act in such a way as to contradict his own holy nature. He cannot, for example, lie or sin or change his holy nature, or break a promise.[2]

So God's power is an *unimpeachable* power, being perfect and beyond criticism, reproach or censure, because it is never unjust, unkind or ungodlike. Human power corrupts, leading to arrogance, extortion, war and a host of other evils, but, as we have just noted, God's acts of power are always in line with his holiness and justice.

We may add that God's power is a *constructive* power, because there is always a purpose or an end in view. By his great power Jesus Christ came into the world and survived an eternal weight of punishment, making atonement for countless sinners. That manifestation of power was a constructive act of mercy, achieving salvation for believers throughout the world, for all eternity. Allied to this, God's

---

2   *2 Corinthians 1.20; Hebrews 6.17-18; Titus 1.2*

power is a morally reforming power, bringing about in the lives of people conviction of sin, repentance, and new life which hungers and thirsts for righteousness. Every one of our Lord's miracles was an act of power with a purpose, namely his personal authentication as the incarnate God, and a demonstration of how he would heal souls.

Even the power of God's anger in judgement will be constructive, because the new and heavenly order will be preserved from all further pain and havoc by the removal of sin. By God's constructive, life-giving power comes the melting of the hard unregenerate heart, the new birth, the giving of a new nature and spiritual life that brings men and women into communion with himself. What a glorious privilege it is to serve the mighty God whose power is so great, so pure and so varied in its application! All human powers and governments of all centuries, even compounded together, are nothing by comparison with the astonishing power of God. And only God's power is inexhaustible.

The Knowledge and Wisdom of God

God's knowledge is the second in this survey of his reflected or communicable attributes, and it is so spectacular that there are many observations to be made. Knowledge has been defined as observation and recognition. It is the understanding and remembering of things. Even animals lacking any substantial power of reason have a degree of knowledge, but human knowledge is obviously far higher. God's knowledge is vastly higher still, being a total and infallible knowledge. By his *knowledge*, God knows everything, and by his *wisdom* he acts perfectly wisely in the use of his knowledge.[3] In human affairs people may be highly qualified in knowledge, and foolish in their

---

3 *1 Samuel 2.3; Psalm 33.13; Psalm 94.9-11; Psalm 104.24; Proverbs 8.22-30; Isaiah 40.13-14; Romans 11.33-36; Hebrews 4.13*

use of what they know. How may we conceive the scope and size of God's knowledge and wisdom?

If we consider the human mind as a speck of dust in the vast expanse of the universe, the contrast is still inadequate for picturing the immensity of God's knowledge by comparison with ours. Here are some comparisons that may help in the quest for a worthy apprehension of the extraordinary knowledge of the Creator.

Unlike our puny knowledge, God's is a *never-learned* knowledge, because he has always known all things, whereas we struggle to acquire and remember every ounce of understanding.

Unlike ours, God's knowledge is *intuitively* known to him. He has no theories, nor does he need to carry out experiments, because knowledge and Truth is his nature. It has been said that God knows by genius, not by toil, and that he knows by genesis, not by analysis.[4]

Unlike ours, God's knowledge is a *perfect, all-seeing* knowledge, there being nothing at all that he does not know. We cannot read thoughts, but God can. We frequently miss the real truth, but God's view of things is always altogether accurate.

Our knowledge is a flickering flame when it looks into the past, and even worse when it peers into the future. God's knowledge, by contrast, is a *knowledge of all eternity*, including all history. With him there is no difference between old and new things, prior or subsequent events, because he sees past, present and future at the same time. We cannot predict the future, not even imminent weather changes, with guaranteed accuracy, but God knows every detail about every nation and every individual into the distant future to the end of time.

God's knowledge is even greater, for *he knows all the things which could have happened* if any circumstance in any chain of events had been different. In this respect God's knowledge is like an infinitely

---

4 'By genesis' means God brings knowledge into being.

vast chessboard. In chess, the skill lies in being able to perceive all the possibilities open to each player as the result of any move, and what further possibilities will arise when any possible move is taken. God knows every situation or event which might have been. If the losing side in a war had actually won it, what course would subsequent events have taken? In what way would the record of history be different? God knows not only the things that happen, but also the staggering number of alternative possibilities.

It is often pointed out that to know oneself is the most fundamental aspect of knowledge, and God's knowledge includes *perfect understanding of himself*. The lack of self-knowledge produces in mankind a pathetic spectacle of people who know about so many things, and yet know so little about their own nature and destiny. Most of the time we cannot discern the deeper motives for the things we do, and we certainly do not see many of our faults. Tragically, people frequently have no perception of their spiritual lifelessness. This is the measure of our simplicity, but God knows himself perfectly, always knowing exactly what he will do, and why, and when, throughout all eternity.

God's knowledge, being so much higher than ours, is also *constant*. We have noted that he sees all things, past, present and future, at the same time, but it must be added that he sees and knows these things *all the time*, because his infinite memory is always operating. He never sleeps or falls into unconsciousness, and he never forgets. It is obviously impossible for us to have a view of all the things that we know all the time. Things drift in and out of our conscious grasp, but God has all his infinite knowledge in his thought perpetually, without a moment's exception.

God's knowledge is completely *impartial*, unlike ours, because he is not subject to any prejudice and is able to judge all matters perfectly. He is never swayed or dazzled by human misrepresentation or concealment. We are constantly swayed by feelings, so that we forgive those we love and condemn those we hate; viewing some things through rose-tinted spectacles, and others through heavily darkened prejudices. As we feel, so we see, but God's knowledge is far above such imperfections.

God's knowledge is perpetually a *concerned* knowledge, whereas human beings show little or no concern over countless tragedies. Starving or injured people are shown on television in some faraway place, and if there is any concern at all it is short-lived; but God is deeply concerned about all that he sees. He sees our acts, together with the earthly and eternal consequences of those acts, and is never indifferent, but always moved with compassion. He is the pleading God who calls hell-bound men and women to repentance, feeling so deeply for us that he has provided a Saviour to suffer and die for us. To all who repent, this concerned knowledge of God is recognised as a deeply affectionate, personal, listening, forgiving and reconciling knowledge.

God's knowledge is a *demonstrated* knowledge, by contrast with ours. We take an examination and either fail or pass with only a percentage of the highest possible mark, so demonstrating the inadequacy of our knowledge. But the perfections of God's knowledge have been demonstrated to the human race in numerous ways. He has, for example, provided in his Word many remarkable and detailed prophecies of future events, a large number of which have already been perfectly fulfilled, demonstrating his accurate knowledge about the ongoing history of humanity.

God has made promises to change the lives of those who trust in him, and these also have been perfectly fulfilled, demonstrating that he knows exactly how to solve the troubles of individuals. The advice of newspaper agony aunts fails constantly, many of these 'experts' failing in their own lives, showing up the poverty of their knowledge of human needs. The knowledge of God has been wonderfully demonstrated to be reliable and true.

Leaving behind the vast difference between puny human knowledge and that of Almighty God, two final observations highlight the impact of God's knowledge upon those who seek after him. When the Holy Spirit first works in the hearts of people they become astonished at what God knows about them, and realise with alarm that all things are 'naked and opened unto the eyes of him with whom we have to do'. It suddenly becomes clear that he knows their every move, every thought, and every sin. We call this 'conviction of sin'. Before this experience, we think only superficially about God and his attributes, but with the dawning of personal salvation comes the first, sometimes shocking, awareness of the searching sight of the living God, and this leads to repentance and submission to him. From that time, the knowledge of God becomes *magnificent*, deeply *enjoyable* and *satisfying*.

For God to share with mortals merely a fraction of what he knows and sees (through the Scriptures) lifts the soul higher than mortal knowledge could ever do. In God's Word we have satisfying explanations of the human condition, heart-stirring presentations of the divine remedy, soaring views of our Lord and Saviour Jesus Christ and his atoning work for sinners, records of the history of redemption, and the awesome revealing of God's plans and purposes for the remainder of time and for eternity. When Christian people explore this revelation it becomes to them even more wonderful than the greatest music or the most breathtaking place of natural beauty. It is nothing other than a portion of the infinite and eternal knowledge of Almighty God.

God is True and Faithful

God is true in three main senses. First, he is perfectly truthful. Secondly, he is entirely logical and rational in his being and views. And thirdly, he *is* the Truth, or the reason or purpose behind life – the explanation for all things.[5] God is the ultimate reality. If anyone

---

5   *Numbers 23.19; Deuteronomy 32.4; Psalm 33.4; Psalm 57.3, 10; Psalm 89.14; Psalm 91.4; John 1.14; John 14.16-17; Romans 3.4, 7.*

searches for the meaning of the universe, everything begins and ends with God, who created all things for himself.

God is the Truth also in the sense that he is absolutely and perfectly right, never having any contradiction or inconsistency in his nature or words or actions. In addition, he is *all* the Truth, because there is nothing further to know, aside from what God knows. Everything that he has revealed in the Scriptures is true, because no lie or mistaken idea has ever been uttered by him. He is the everlasting and inexhaustible Truth, and in Heaven the ransomed people shall learn of him throughout eternity without ever encountering anything false or misleading.

Finally, God is the Truth when he tells the human race the absolute truth about its guilt and condemnation, and about the way of salvation through Christ Jesus. Many psychologists maintain there is no such thing as a sinful person, and society engages in non-stop self-flattery, but God always speaks reality and tells the truth.

God's truthfulness includes his faithfulness. He makes many promises, including the promises of salvation, and because these are made truthfully they will surely be kept. God uses no double-speak, has no contradictory hidden agenda or motives, and will never double-cross or act contrary to his revealed Word. Neither will he ever change his opinions or his intentions.[6]

By contrast there is not much truth and faithfulness in human affairs. Agreements are constantly broken and the debris of unfulfilled promises is strewn high across the road of life. As fallen and limited creatures we change our plans, tastes and allegiances constantly, but God never does. We forget our promises, regret having made them, and try to escape them, but God never acts in this way. Spin and fraud is commonplace in politics and business, while marriages collapse as people act disloyally to those to whom

---

6   *Deuteronomy 7.8-9; 2 Samuel 23.5; 1 Chronicles 28.20; Psalm 36.5; Psalm 40.10; Lamentations 3.23; Matthew 24.34; 1 Corinthians 1.9; 2 Corinthians 1.20.*

they once pledged faithfulness. A thousand and one unreliable claims and philosophies hang like thick smog in the air, but God's unfailing faithfulness remains an attribute of infinite comfort and security.

God's faithfulness is an *observant* faithfulness, because he watches closely all the affairs of his children, who are never out of his sight and care. A person seriously injured in a remote place may die for lack of attention, but the Lord, who never slumbers or sleeps, sees all things and is always open to the prayers of his people, responding in the wisest way. The Israelites of old complained about their national trials saying, 'My way is hid from the Lord, and my judgment is passed over from my God,' but Isaiah reproved them in those famous words: 'Hast thou not heard, that the everlasting God, the Lord, the Creator of the ends of the earth, fainteth not, neither is weary? there is no searching *[no discoverable limit]* of his understanding.'[7] When Saul of Tarsus sat blind in Damascus, the Lord saw and said to Ananias, 'Behold, he prayeth.'

God's faithfulness is also *lively* and *immediate*. While he holds many blessings in store for a future time, he also deals kindly with his people whenever they call upon him. In human situations a doctor may take a long time to come, and a builder will take considerably longer. Any appeal to the courts for some legal redress could take months or years, and there are long waiting periods in other areas of life, but the Lord's faithfulness is expressed speedily. This is seen best in the experience of conversion, which is not a lifelong process but an immediate work of God when the heart is opened and the Gospel sincerely embraced.

God's faithfulness is a *proven* faithfulness. Christians unite in testimony to his faithfulness in keeping the promises of salvation, and his promises about the blessings of the Christian life. God's faithfulness is proved supremely in the coming of Christ to atone for sinners

---

7　*Isaiah 40.27-28*

on Calvary's cross in accordance with centuries of prophecy, and we look forward to the sure realisation of promised events at the return of Christ, and the end of the age.

4

The Reflected Attributes of God

Goodness – Love – Holiness – Justice

'The Lord is gracious, and full of compassion;
slow to anger, and of great mercy' *(Psalm 145.8).*

The Goodness and Love of God

KING DAVID SAID – 'Oh how great is thy goodness . . . which thou hast wrought for them that trust in thee before the sons of men!'[1] God's goodness reveals the immeasurable beauty of his nature, showing particularly his benevolence and compassion, while his love shows how he feels for people, and the affection he has for the redeemed. Goodness is the foundation of his love, and a most active attribute, being constantly deployed in acts of mercy, kindness and longsuffering.[2] Because he is good, God forgives, supplies, protects and sustains the objects of his love. To think about God's

---

1 *Psalm 31.19*
2 *Exodus 33.19; Psalm 106.1; Psalm 107; Romans 8.28*

goodness and love in a devotional rather than scientific manner, we offer the following eight ways of viewing this sublime characteristic.

1 God's goodness is an *intrinsic* and *natural* goodness. People have to cultivate lovingkindness, but in God it exists naturally. In us it needs to be stimulated, sometimes by affection or kindness being shown to us, or by our being emotionally moved by something, such as the plight of a helpless child. God's goodness, by contrast, needs no stimulation.

We frequently and easily lose any small amount of goodness or love that is within us, especially when anger, resentment, jealousy, or even hatred and malice displaces it, but God's goodness is unaffected by any such things. It is his nature.

2 God's goodness is a *reproducing* goodness, because he is the source and fountain of all other goodness found in this world. He lends it to human nature, and people who die in a state of rebellion against him will find all traces of goodness taken from them in the day of judgement. When this earthly 'Babylon' falls, the sound of good things 'shall be heard no more at all in thee'.[3]

God imparts a measure of goodness even to rebellious sinners to keep the world bearable. If he did not do so, the world would become such a hotbed of violence and hate that no human being could exist in it. God also imparts a measure of goodness to rebellious people in order that sin may be more clearly defined by contrast. Seams of goodness throw sin into stark relief, and we see our depravity.

God also imparts a measure of goodness and love in this fallen world to provide a language for the Gospel. How could we understand the love and compassion of God in providing salvation if we never saw a trace of love in human affairs? Kindness and mercy would be concepts totally unknown among us, but God leaves goodness in this world even among the debris of sin so that the message

---

3   *Revelation 18.22-23*

of his great goodness may be recognised, and the blessings of salvation valued and embraced.

3 God's goodness is *ancient*, dating from everlasting. It was generously displayed in the Garden of Eden when all good things were given to our first parents, and it was shown again in the glorious promise of a Saviour given to them when they rebelled. From the dawn of life on Earth God has been approachable to men and women, and his pardoning love available.

Idol-gods invented by human minds have nearly always been capricious, greedy, vicious and tyrannical. They supposedly receive sacrifices from their worshippers on a 'protection racket' basis, needing placation to do them any good. God's original goodness is vastly better.

The true God has shown his goodness to the world in another way also, by moving the church to introduce into society great works of compassion, such as hospitals, care of the poor, abolition of slavery, and a host of other compassionate acts. Slowly over the last century the world has learned from the church the obligation of care. A leading scientist recently speaking in favour of atheism in a major scientific conference in the USA, acknowledged ruefully that the religious community gave far more money for relief after Hurricane Katrina than the government. He then acknowledged that no secular scientific groups had donated anything.[4]

4 Among the many facets of God's goodness is his extraordinary *longsuffering*, for he has been sorely tempted and tried across the centuries by idolatry, animism, atheism, materialism, and human self-confidence. He has looked upon generations of people who would not have him to reign over them, and who ignored, derided, slandered and hated him. Yet he has determined that many millions

---

4   *New Scientist*, 18 November, 2006, page 11.

of people through the history of the world will seek him, find him, and enter into life.

Think of how God bore with the indifference of the children of Israel for almost two millennia, holding back punishment and sending prophets to plead and implore before finally implementing his warnings. What earthly potentate has ever treated rebels with such longsuffering?

It is often noted how God bore with the sins of Bible characters both good and bad, tolerating, for example, Job's insolence, Jacob's deceitfulness, Solomon's lust, Hezekiah's pride, and, for a long time, Manasseh's massive crimes. He bore also with the persecuting malice of Saul of Tarsus, and with so many others who offended against him and tried to thwart his purposes.

Many Christians remember how God bore with their faltering, wavering, hesitating steps to repent, at the time of their conversion. He graciously overlooked their inclination to choose the pleasures of this world, and he tolerated their insulting resistance to his call, patiently drawing them to himself for mercy.

God's longsuffering goodness is seen in the scale of blessing he continues to pour out upon believers despite their waywardness. Unstintingly he gives forgiveness, light, communion and a thousand evidences to assure of salvation. He bestows gifts, helps, guidance and encouragement without ration or measure, his goodness being continuous and inexhaustible. Human society rewards its struggling members with inequality, hardship, and even tumult and war, but God's goodness to his people is far above all comparison. It is unmatched.

5 Lest we should think that God, in his power and glory, is like an infinitely gigantic computer, functioning far above human sensitivities, we must affirm that his goodness is an intensely *feelingful* goodness. God is not like an insurance company which pays out in response to a claim but has no personal concern for those

who suffer. Nor is God like a secretary of state in charge of social security who cannot be expected to personally identify with the trials of those in need. The Lord's goodness carries with it deep personal concern for those he helps, 'For as the heaven is high above the earth, so great is his mercy toward them that fear him . . . Like as a father pitieth his children, so the Lord pitieth them that fear him. For he knoweth our frame; he remembereth that we are dust.'[5]

God's goodness smiles with affection as he deals directly with praying souls. He bids us cast all our care upon him, for he cares for us,[6] and he assures us that: 'we have not an high priest which cannot be touched with the feeling of our infirmities.'[7]

6 Living as we do in a world of continuous social flux, and surrounded by change and decay, it is glorious to observe that God's goodness is a *consistent* goodness. We vary so greatly in our bursts of goodwill to others. In society at large we discriminate from person to person, and even in the family we may vary in the expression of goodness from child to child. Our goodness also varies according to our mood while God, by contrast, lavishes his goodness in salvation without ebb or flow to all who call upon him.

Our outflowing goodness is so often eroded by our selfishness and self-consideration, being spoiled by the nasty side of human nature, and we see this inconsistency very clearly in others. The closer we draw to a person we admire, the more we see the slenderness of that person's real goodness. Many old sayings illustrate this, for no knight is a hero to his page, no master is a gentleman in the eyes of his valet, and no officer is a man of honour to his batman. The good and the great begin to be 'debunked' almost as soon as they die.

How limited is human goodness, yet how consistent and unabating

5   *Psalm 103.11-14*
6   *1 Peter 5.7*
7   *Hebrews 4.15*

is the Lord's! How tragic it is when we make ourselves enemies of the God of great goodness.

7 We cannot omit the fact that God's goodness is an entirely *gracious* and *undeserved* goodness, and this is the basis of our salvation. The benefits of divine love cannot be earned. From the foundation of the world no one has deserved the kindness of the Lord, so God has made it unconditional and free. By contrast, our goodness seldom flows from entirely gracious benevolence, but is mostly shown for gain, or, as we have already pointed out, in exchange for equal goodwill from other people. We tend to express love toward those who show us (or are likely to show us) friendship, favours, helpfulness, or who are similar to us in age, personality or tastes. God, however, gives his love freely, bestowing pardon for sin, kindness for rebellion, new life for spiritual inertia, communion for alienation, honour for contempt, and love for hatred. All his blessings come because of his gracious goodness.

8 Finally, in this catalogue of some aspects of God's goodness, we admire it because it is a *sacrificial* goodness. We tend to make limited and painless sacrifices in order to do good to others, our 'goodness' seldom costing much, except in the case of those very close to us. God's goodness and love for those who have been objectionable in his sight is seen in the mission of our Lord and Saviour Jesus Christ, who, though the Creator of all, took upon himself human nature and gave himself to great humiliation and the incomprehensible agony of atonement, for our salvation. How far would the Saviour's goodness go to redeem his people? The eternal Son of God, equal with the Father, went all the way to Calvary, demonstrating his immensely sacrificial goodness.

A reflection of God's sacrificial goodness is seen in the history of the church, in the lives of those who seek to reflect the divine character. We see the price paid by martyr-preachers down the ages, and by the early missionaries, who gave themselves to a premature death for the sake of reaching lost men and women with the message of salvation. Christ's people are still to be seen sacrificing their time and resources to bring salvation to neighbourhoods throughout the world, even should they be sorely persecuted for their efforts. God has touched their hearts with his own sacrificial goodness so that they acquire that *giving* tendency that accepts trial and hardship to bring compassion to others.

* * *

God's goodness and love are infinite, intrinsic, natural, original, existing from of old, longsuffering, feelingful, consistent, gracious and sacrificial. They flow to unworthy people in the form of grace and compassion. They create good things, provide sources of pleasure, supply the needs of the world, relieve pain and answer prayer. Sin has entered in to cut humanity off from the full expression of God's goodness and love, yet these still break through to men and women in many ways, most of all in salvation, and the time is coming when a regenerated, rejuvenated world peopled by those who love Christ will know these attributes in unobscured and limitless measure.

The Holiness and Justice of God

So great is the gulf between the vestigial shreds of holiness found in the human race, and the purity of God, that we have little ability to comprehend perfect holiness. There is something very distinctive about God's holiness over all his other attributes because it describes his essential character. If we may speak very broadly and imprecisely, some attributes tend to describe his 'size' (such as his infinity, knowledge and power) while others describe how he acts (such as love, goodness and truthfulness). One attribute provides just a glimpse of his mysterious 'substance' (that he is divine spirit), but the word *holiness* draws all the attributes together and declares that God is perfect and pure in himself. He is not only without sin, but he is infinitely virtuous and righteous. Therefore, in *holiness* we see something of his glorious *overall* nature or personality or character.

The Hebrew and Greek words used in the Bible for holiness mean *separateness*, or even *unreachability*. Such words are used of God in the context of a fallen sinful world, to show that he is so pure and so righteous that he is far distant from sin. He loves good and hates evil. He is pure and unblemished in his nature, thoughts, plans, actions and words.

When Adam and Eve disobeyed God, renouncing trust in him alone, and choosing instead to acquire the knowledge and experience of good and evil, a mighty gulf of separation rose between them and their Creator. God withdrew and stood aloof, far from them.

The word 'separate' as a term for God's holiness also tells us that God is *exclusively* perfect: 'There is none holy as the Lord: for there is none beside thee,' prayed Hannah.[8] 'Holiness' tells us that God's love, goodness, benevolence, truthfulness, compassion, kindness, faithfulness and fairness are all colours of a sublime spectrum that blend together as radiant purity. This is God's unchanging, unfading, untarnished beauty, that will never be challenged, and which blazes forth with a power and intensity that renders the sun an invisible speck of lifeless dust.

God's holiness made a perfect and holy world before the Fall, and maintains even now a perfect paradise in the heavens for ransomed souls. At the end of the age, at the return of Christ, the power of his holiness will purify, reconstitute and rejuvenate the world for the eternal occupation of his people.[9]

Here are just some of the references to God's holiness in his Word:–

'Who is like unto thee, O Lord . . . glorious in holiness?' *(Exodus 15.11)*

'Holy, holy, holy, is the Lord of hosts' *(Isaiah 6.3)*.

---

8   *1 Samuel 2.2*
9   *Revelation 21.1-2, 10*

'For thou art not a God that hath pleasure in wickedness: neither shall evil dwell with thee' *(Psalm 5.4).*

'For thus saith the high and lofty One that inhabiteth eternity, whose name is Holy . . . ' *(Isaiah 57.15).*

'Thou art of purer eyes than to behold evil, and canst not look on iniquity' *(Habakkuk 1.13).*

'This then is the message which we have heard of him . . . that God is light, and in him is no darkness at all' *(1 John 1.5).*

The Problem of the Justice of God

A longing for justice is deeply etched on human nature, every person feeling indignation when others abuse the rules of society and get away with wrong or criminal behaviour. Even with sinful hearts people constantly judge others.[10]

This strong sense of justice, though frequently hypocritical in sinners, reflects the altogether higher, purer justice of God. God's justice arises from his perfect holiness and his hatred of all that is vile and sinful. He cannot tolerate sin or accommodate it in his presence or in his plan for a new Heaven and a new Earth. His holy nature is committed to the punishment of sin.[11]

Human beings constantly try to lower the standards of judgement, just as present-day society seeks to dispose of God's standards for moral conduct, but God's feelings against sin will never change, and he will see that justice is done at the end of every life.

In the light of personal sin and guilt, how can anyone be accepted by God and blessed? This question leads to another: how can a perfectly righteous and just God, who must punish all sin, have the scope to forgive people, as he must be faithful to his absolutely holy and just nature? How can he be ready to forgive all them that call

---

10 *Romans 2.1-6*
11 *Psalm 7.11; Psalm 9.7-8; Psalm 97.2; Isaiah 5.16; Isaiah 30.18; Daniel 9.14; Nahum 1.3-6; Acts 17.31; Romans 3.5-6.*

upon him?[12] The solution to this, probably the greatest problem in the universe, is prophesied in famous and remarkable words in the *Psalms*:

> **'Mercy and truth are met together; righteousness and peace have kissed each other'** *(Psalm 85.10).*

God's willingness to show *mercy* will be reconciled with his *truth* (his necessity to act absolutely justly) in a solution of divine genius. God's *righteousness* (again referring to his inflexible justice) and his *peace* (his longing to bring about pardon and reconciliation for men and women) will embrace, so that both are satisfied. What will God do to enable him to operate in justice toward people, and yet still forgive them? He will enter the world himself in the person of Jesus Christ, who will go to the cross of Calvary to receive the full and eternal punishment for sin on behalf of all who would look to him for pardon. The atonement accomplished by Christ will enable God's justice and mercy to meet. That great act would enable God to be 'just, and the justifier of him which believeth in Jesus'.[13]

---

12 *Psalm 86.5*
13 *Romans 3.26*

5
The Fall of Man

'Now the serpent . . . said unto the woman, Yea, hath God said,
Ye shall not eat of every tree of the garden?' *(Genesis 3.1)*

THE FALL OF MAN recorded in the opening chapters of the
Bible is the key to understanding human nature and the state
of the world. Apart from this there is no credible explanation
of the human condition, including, for example, the existence of the
human conscience – the awareness of right and wrong that marks
out and lifts people far above the animals. Only the Fall explains
why it is that although we have this built-in moral alarm system we
cannot obey it or maintain the standards it demands. Here is just
one of the mysteries of human nature for which no literature in the
world, aside from the Bible, can account.

Only the Fall explains cruel wars and all other human hostility,
not to mention ubiquitous greed, selfishness, and antagonism to
God. Taking this last point, would it not be reasonable for people to
welcome the idea that there is a good, kind and magnificent Creator,

who is ready to grant communion with himself, and to freely give a vast range of benefits to them, even eternal life? Why then do so many people struggle to prove that there is no God, no afterlife, no standards, and no ultimate good? You cannot explain human nature without the Fall. Nor can you account for the arrival of suffering and tragedy in the world.

Nothing makes sense without this foundational concept of a human race fallen through the 'original sin'. If the biblical record of the Fall was not true history revealed by God, it would still be the most remarkable piece of literature since the beginning of writing, because it mirrors so perfectly what happens in all human behaviour down the centuries. Its apparent simplicity conceals piercing accuracy and profound layers of meaning, showing either divine inspiration, or literary and psychological genius at its very highest. In the event it is presented in the Bible as literal history and attested by Christ as such.

The greatest mistake that anyone can make in religion is to think that he is able to please God by his own achievements of righteousness, an error that comes from having an inadequate grasp of what happened at the Fall of the human race, with the consequent corruption of human character. Only the Bible speaks about the Fall of man and the need of a Saviour. The problem of other faiths is that there is no acceptance of the Fall and of human depravity, and so the idea arises that people are able to satisfy God's requirements by their own meritorious acts, but it cannot be done.[1]

Some may think that the Fall of man is a negative subject, depressing and profoundly pessimistic, but it is the doorway to realism, demonstrating the need for a Saviour, and for an operation of God

---

1   The Koran contains an extremely late version (c AD 600) of the temptation of Adam and his wife but relates their failure as a personal misdemeanour, soon forgiven, and with no consequences for mankind. There is no Fall of mankind, and so redemption is not necessary, and people are able to please God by their own righteous works.

in lives. Despite the many remarkable abilities given to mankind by God, and despite the undoubted achievements of people over the centuries, there is so much to be cynical about in this world. There is so much antagonism to morality, and so much vileness and inhumanity that we must face up to human depravity.

In *Genesis 3*, we look into a 'garden' of indescribable beauty and bliss. Adam and Eve have been created, the human race is underway, and the air is full of purity, happiness, moral power and above all, fellowship with God. The first couple have perfect harmony, and experience every pure and pleasurable sensation known to mankind. Their paradise has no sin, no hurt, no betrayal, no grief, no sorrow, no disappointment, no fear, death or parting, and no pain or weariness – only boundless energy and unlimited intellectual satisfaction, for here is a place under the protective power and the unwavering kindness of Almighty God. Nothing deteriorates or decays in this place of unfading beauty. Yet here is the scene for the worst imaginable moment of treachery. What could possibly have brought this about?

In that paradise a serpent or snake would address Eve. A talking snake? Yes, because Satan, a senior-most angel who had fallen from Heaven through pride,[2] entered into it, this phenomenon not presenting any alarm to Eve who was already used to great wonders and surprises, and had no cause to be suspicious of anything. That snake, in the beginning, would have been an erect and beautiful animal, because before the Fall there was nothing sinister or revolting to be seen.[3] However, this particular animal had been occupied by the enemy of human souls.

At the heart of the Garden, in the midst of numerous fruit trees, were two particularly significant ones, the tree of life, and the tree of knowledge of good and evil. To Eve, Satan said – 'Yea, hath God said,

2   *Luke 10.18; Isaiah 14.12*
3   *Genesis 3.14*

Ye shall not eat of every tree of the garden?'[4] In effect, he asked – 'Has God really said this?' as though to produce in Eve's mind uncertainty about the exact meaning of God's words, and also to create doubt about the reasonableness of God's command.

In response the woman affirmed that they could eat all except one of the fruits in the garden – 'But of the fruit of the tree which is in the midst of the garden, God hath said, Ye shall not eat of it, neither shall ye touch it, lest ye die.'[5] But in relating God's command Eve consciously or otherwise weakened it, because God had said – 'thou *shalt surely* die'.[6] Perhaps she was merely careless, but she turned something definite into something merely possible, and Satan immediately exploited her weakened view, directly contradicting God's words and saying – 'Ye shall *not* surely die.'[7]

What exactly was the fruit of the tree of knowledge of good and evil? It was not an apple, an idea that drifted into vogue from Greek mythology. It was the token or symbol of an alternative world where values and experiences contrary to God's holy standards could be explored and indulged. Such a world did not yet exist, but the instant Adam and Eve exercised the freedom of choice built into their nature, and chose to disobey God, this other world would spring into existence around them, a world where the opposite and negation of every precious thing would be available. A new world of 'anti-values' would, in a sense, be produced by the will of man.

How slippery was the slope to ruin? It was not slippery at all, because God had made it very easy for Adam and Eve to maintain their love and loyalty to their Creator, having given them a perfect nature that delighted in holiness. God had compressed the Ten Commandments with all their deep requirements into one simple duty – Do not choose to know what life would be like without God.

4   *Genesis 3.1*
5   *Genesis 3.3*
6   *Genesis 2.17*
7   *Genesis 3.4*

Our first parents had wonderful freedom of intellect, and all happiness, resting on this single requirement of obedience – Obey me and trust me by never taking that fruit.

Having denied that Adam and Eve would die by eating the forbidden fruit, the serpent then attributed to God a base and jealous motive, saying that God knew that 'in the day ye eat thereof, then your eyes shall be opened, and ye shall be as gods, knowing good and evil.'[8]

'Take the fruit and you will be just like God,' said Satan, implying that God was barring their access to something even more desirable, where they would have still greater liberty, and equality with the Creator. God was keeping things from them.

Sin began there in the Garden of Eden when Eve chose to believe the lie, wanting something more, something else, and becoming ready to distrust God and defy him in order to have what she wanted. But was not Eve just a simple, naïve girl, duped by Satan and momentarily tripped by temptation? Was she not a childish innocent who was subsequently over-punished for being the victim of a lie?[9]

We know that Eve was not only beautiful but also, like Adam, powerfully intelligent, because God said of all his creative work, 'behold, it was very good.'[10] Never, until the coming of Jesus Christ, were humility and intellectual powers so marvellously combined. We may be sure of her high intelligence for another reason also, because as the first image-bearers and ancestors of the entire human race, Adam and Eve would have possessed qualities to the highest degree. They bore the original genes from which all people would be formed, the only variations after the Fall being imperfections rather

---

8 *Genesis 3.5*
9 The great theologians of the past spoke of the Garden of Eden as the time of man's 'innocence' but they did not mean naivety. They referred only to his being created free from all evil, prior to the Fall.
10 *Genesis 1.31*

than improvements. Bearing in mind that the origin of all natural gifts lay in Adam and Eve, we may be sure that they grasped the issues of their temptation with penetrating clarity before they made their fatal choice.

Sin began, therefore, moments before the fruit was actually taken, and not one offence, but many uniting together in a compound sin of horrific proportions. 'What a small thing!' say cynics, 'that the entire future of the human race should turn on one small act of disobedience – the taking of a single fruit!' But you may just as well describe the harrowing destructive force unleashed on Hiroshima or Nagasaki as the result of a mere 'fission-trigger'. We do not look only at the taking and eating of the fruit, but all that lay immediately behind it. We do not look at the finger pulling the trigger, but into the mind that determined the deed.

We see in our first parents a rapid surge of sinful attitudes, all original and unprecedented, and all generated and permitted by their will; by their free, uncoerced liberty of choice. We see an amalgam of ingratitude, unbelief, disloyalty and pride, and still we have not exhausted the sins behind the crime.

Pride said, 'This is what I am entitled to and ought to have, and God is unreasonably keeping it from me,' and so the human race looked away from God, and all the opposite values, the anti-values, came into being. They were never in man's world before that terrible moment, but Eve and then Adam chose them. They effectively said, with utmost defiance, 'We hereby turn away from our Creator,' and the opposites of life, love, purity and beauty entered in.

If Eve chose first, Adam was worse, needing no direct approach by Satan. It has been said that *she* was tempted and *he* fell, but it is impossible and irrelevant to attribute levels of blame. Adam, it seems, wholly and unreservedly endorsed Eve's proposal to eat.

The full horror of their compound sin is laid bare in the biblical narrative, especially the motives of Eve. We read: 'When the woman saw that the tree was good for food, and that it was pleasant to the eyes, and a tree to be desired to make one wise, she took of the fruit thereof, and did eat, and gave also unto her husband with her; and he did eat.'[11] It appears from the record that God's warning was weighed against her desire, and rejected. To Eve it was all a matter of what was good to taste, good in appearance, and good for an entirely new field of knowledge. God had pronounced that fruit bad, so bad it would kill them, but Eve (then Adam) chose to believe the contrary, that it was very good and would confer upon them a new and desirable status.

We observe this in our present-day society, where God's values are flagrantly swept aside in favour of what people want to do to satisfy their various lusts and selfish aspirations. If God has pronounced something to be death-producing, man eventually legalises and flaunts it.

The desires of Eve are expressed in the New Testament in these words: 'For all that is in the world, the lust of the flesh, and the lust of the eyes, and the pride of life, is not of the Father, but is of the world.'[12] These desires were launched by Satan in the Garden of Eden to bring down the human race, and they continue to be his central threefold strategy of temptation.

Eve heard, considered and agreed with Satan's lie, took the fruit, and ate – a series of distinctive acts. Similarly Adam, in distinctive acts, received the fruit from her, and ate. These steps or stages are informative, pointing to the thoughtful, premeditated nature of their act. From the moment Eve weighed the words of the serpent, contemplated the forbidden fruit and wanted its supposed benefits, up to the moment she plucked that fruit, a period of seconds or more passed, during which a cluster of sins developed like an avalanche. The moments between plucking and eating also show the settled determination of her disobedience. Eve was not artlessly swept by

---

11 *Genesis 3.6*
12 *1 John 2.16*

deception into an impulsive act, but she acted very deliberately in line with her free choice. It was a wilful act in which she decided to set God aside and disobey him.

We have already noted that the response of both Adam and Eve to Satan involved the following sins: ingratitude toward God, unbelief, disloyalty, and pride. But now, the actual taking and eating of the fruit added disobedience, rebellion and capitulation to lust, placing the human race in total opposition to God's will and rule.

Our parents had been created perfect and holy, and given the closest imaginable association with their God. Sin did not lurk in their minds or hearts even in embryonic form, nor were they simpletons, unable to discern the implications of Satan's lie. But they chose to believe the lie, and from that moment sin was born, leading to the moment of eating, when 'the eyes of them both were opened, and they knew that they were naked.'[13] All the ugliness of lust now became known to them, because their natures had become corrupt, and their glorious purity and holiness shattered.

At that moment death came into their lives, just as they had been warned; a twofold death. They died *spiritually*, because their close communion with God had been destroyed, and they would in future be outside his kingdom, kindness and rule. They had become enemies of God, and very shortly would be fugitives.

They had also died *physically*, for although their bodies were still alive, the process of physical death had begun, and their days would be limited by the course of ageing and death.

All too soon the alienated pair – 'heard the voice of the Lord God walking in the garden in the cool of the day: and Adam and his wife hid themselves.' They could no longer walk there without fear, because guilt now formed a foreboding barrier between them and God. However, sin had not finished its work of ruin, because despite guilt and fear they quickly denied their wrongs, embarking

---

13 *Genesis 3.7*

on a course of self-justification. God drew near, but they did not seek him. God spoke, yet they made no response. Then the Creator's voice rang through the Garden – 'Where art thou?'[14]

God, of course, knew where they were, because he knows everything, his words being a challenge rather than a question. Adam replied: 'I heard thy voice in the garden, and I was afraid, because I was naked; and I hid myself.'

'Who told thee that thou wast naked?' asked the searching, convicting voice of God, giving Adam the opportunity to confess all. 'Hast thou eaten of the tree, whereof I commanded thee that thou shouldest not eat?' Adam still would not repent, but first blamed Eve, and then God himself, for giving him a wife. His blaming of Eve was the first act of betrayal and of disloyalty by one person of another in human history. 'The woman whom thou gavest to be with me, she gave me of the tree, and I did eat.'

This dialogue constitutes the most accurate description ever penned of the continuing self-delusion of the human race. We sin, but it is not our fault, rather the fault of our upbringing, or our environment, or what other people have done to us. In today's victim culture the 'blame game' gets worse and worse, because pride rules, preventing people from accepting responsibility for almost any wrongdoing.

In the case of Adam and Eve the entire spectrum of human sin flooded in because Satan's lie was preferred above God's truth, and self-gratification above obedience. Yet Adam did not at first grasp the horror of his fall, nor its implications, and neither do we. Until we realise the great gulf between ourselves and God, and our offensiveness to him, we cannot properly seek him. Only a clear view of the extent of the Fall and the sinfulness of the human heart prepares people for true repentance before God.

There is every likelihood that Adam and Eve did repent

---

14 *Genesis 3.9*

subsequently, although this is not stated in the biblical record. But while still in the Garden Adam blamed Eve, and she blamed the serpent.

Through the Fall physical death arrived, all biology changed, 'nature, red in tooth and claw' marked the loss of God's special favour, and the era of toil and trouble arrived. Mankind chose life outside God's goodness, and just such an environment swept in. But God's sentence was not without an amazing promise, for he said to the serpent: 'I will put enmity between thee and the woman, and between thy seed and her seed; it shall bruise thy head, and thou shalt bruise his heel.'[15]

A glorious descendant of Adam and Eve would one day come, who would bruise or crush the serpent's head. God spoke, of course, of Christ, the second person of the Trinity, who would come to Earth by incarnation and go to Calvary's cross to make atonement for sin on behalf of all who trusted in him. The crime of Satan in bringing down the human race would lead to Christ sustaining indescribable suffering (pictured as *his* 'heel' being crushed or bruised), but being divine as well as human he would rise again from the dead.

Without knowing the enormity of the sin of the Fall, we cannot see the mountainous barrier between ourselves and God. Without the Fall, we can never really understand the Cross. Only the Fall enables us to see the tragedy and sinfulness of wilful human choice, and the infinite kindness and mercy of Christ the Saviour in coming to secure forgiveness and new life for billions of people throughout the history of the world.

We have observed that in the narrative of the Fall there are explanations for human attitudes throughout time, because the tempter's strategies never change, and human beings repeat the responses of their first parents. Just as Satan sowed doubts in

---

15 *Genesis 3.15*

the mind of Eve about God and his commands, he continues to do with people today. He does not want anyone to believe in a God who may be trusted or who has total authority over them. He does not mind people having a lesser god, but not the true God. Accordingly he asks – has God really laid down standards for people to live by? Are they really going to be punished by him when they die? No! – says Satan – people should reject such ideas, believing they have a right to do whatever they please as long as others are not injured.

'God is keeping you down and keeping things from you,' insinuated Satan to Eve, and he continues this theme today, saying, 'Religion is unreasonable and restrictive; push beyond morality; be as God; be your own God.'

Although God had said to Eve that one particular fruit was deadly, she decided it was good for food. She also considered it beautiful to view, and highly desirable for the obtaining of outlawed knowledge. The instant she mistrusted God, rebellious thinking gathered in strength, and so it is with us. Dismiss the Bible and the Ten Commandments, and all moral restraints quickly fall, lusts assert themselves and the new liberalised society gets rapidly worse. As with Eve, appearances matter more than character, and the longing for things comes before any quest for meaning and purpose in life.

We say, 'I don't want God because he is unfair, restrictive, and cruel. I will not listen to him or obey him. I don't believe his threat of punishment or death, and when I die I'm sure I will go to Heaven – if there is such a place.' The latter presumption started in the Garden of Eden, showing the arrogance that rapidly forms with the onset of disobedience to God.

Sin is vile to God, utterly unreasonable, and destructive in every possible way. Since Eden, human nature has continued in depravity, and apart from the possibility of forgiveness through Christ, all people live and die under the warning of death.

Human depravity does not exclude all goodness as we have pointed out in an earlier chapter, because God has determined that positive traits and feelings will remain in some measure even in corrupt and disobedient hearts, so that the world will not become utterly unbearable, and also to give people time in life to repent. All that we do, however, is deeply tainted by the Fall.

Selfish and proud desires and motives permeate everything we do, and this is why the world is as it is, and strife and heartache pursue us even in the happiest phases of life. The emotional roller coaster of life portrayed in television soaps is a true view of humanity, except that they dare not bring in the full reality of violence, deprivation, immorality and misery that prevails throughout the world.

The biblical doctrine of 'total depravity' does not mean that people are 100% evil, but that they are stained and corrupted in every department of mind, heart and will. Pride inevitably objects to this, but it cannot be denied. Man's Fall is the reason for every horrible aspect of life in the world throughout history, and without the love of Christ and the salvation he brings, we would be utterly without hope and without God in the world.

The Fall is the reason for a world in which disease and death terminates lives often with great suffering, snatching even babies and children from happiness, and bringing down their parents in grief. Original sin brought about the Fall, and our wilful, continuing godlessness endorses the step of our first parents.

Where is God in tragedy and sorrow? He is found by individuals who seek Christ and his pardoning love. Through Christ we receive reconciliation with God, new life, new purpose, strength from on high, and eternal security. With this new life parents may surround their grievously sick children with love for God, nurturing in them the same trust in Christ and certainty of eternity, so that sickness and death become the gateway to Heaven, and God is trusted and praised for his great salvation.

6

The Three Dark Hours of Calvary
Eight Purposes and Lessons

'Now from the sixth hour there was darkness over all the land
unto the ninth hour' *(Matthew 27.45)*.

THE CRUCIFIXION OF CHRIST took place on a hillside
called 'the place of a skull'. It began at 9am, the scene being
bathed in daylight until noon, when suddenly total darkness
descended, lasting until 3pm. This deep darkness covered all the
land of Judea (at least[1]) and cannot be explained in natural terms.
It was not an eclipse of the sun, because the crucifixion occurred at
the time of the Passover, which always coincided with a full moon.
It was not a sirocco, the insufferably hot wind which carried sand
and frequently obscured the light, because this would probably have

---

1 The Greek could be translated 'over all the Earth', but this is unlikely as
half the Earth would have been in darkness anyway, and, probably, in God's
'economy' this miracle would be intended only for those who knew what was
happening.

been noted by Matthew, and would not, in any case, have resulted in complete darkness. The extinguishing of the light of the sun was nothing less than an act of God, Christian writers of the past taking the view that it was a miracle performed directly by Christ, despite his dying weakness.

The dramatic failure of light undoubtedly struck fear into the hearts of the watching crowd, the Jews having been schooled in prophecies of warning, which told of a coming judgement in which the sun would be darkened.

It was certainly appropriate that all nature, created by the Lord, should be compelled to bow her head when he carried out his work on Calvary's cross. It was as if the sun paused in tribute and human activity was commanded to halt. Among the people apprehension and awe prevailed, and all insults were silenced. The words of Isaac Watts convey the impact of the darkness during the most amazing transaction in the history of the world –

> Well might the sun in darkness hide,
> And shut his glories in,
> When Christ, the mighty Maker, died
> For man the creature's sin.

But what exactly did the darkness signify? Why did it occur? What did it say to humanity? What aspects of Christ's atoning work could be highlighted by three mysterious hours of imposed night? Here are eight reasons why a mantle of blindness fell upon the vast crowd that came to see the execution of the Saviour.

1. Christ's Divine Dignity Marked

For three long hours the Lord suffered visible torment in full view of thousands, ample time for historical attestation of the fact that he had truly entered human flesh and suffered. Then, exactly halfway through the ordeal, a veil was drawn across the scene on account of his noble station. The darkness did not lessen his suffering, but paid tribute to his Godhead. His dignity and his glory were so great that defiled eyes would not be permitted to stare at his humiliation for longer than was necessary. One might say that Christ's *visible* humiliation was curtailed to signal his divine greatness.

2. Christ's Extreme Pain Concealed

As the hours passed, the mental and physical anguish of the Lord caused by his bearing an eternal weight of punishment on behalf of millions, must have tortured his face and racked his frame to a hideous degree. The full extent of his deformity would be hidden from public view.

However, an even greater reason for the darkness was that outward appearances could never show the real nature of Christ's suffering. If we were to be transported back to Calvary to see him there, we would not be able to evaluate the hidden inner pain of his anguish. His appearance could never convey just how much he bore.

We may think of the eternal woe compressed unimaginably into the space of six hours, and the incomprehensible impact of guilt and punishment upon a holy, sinless soul. The three hours of darkness teach that a suffering far beyond anything that could be seen or measured was being borne at Calvary. Movies purporting to depict Christ's passion can show only physical suffering at the most, but his physical pains were infinitesimal by comparison with his affliction of soul when he experienced separation from the Father on our behalf. A film can only detract from the real nature of his agonies, giving an impression of Christ's extreme physical torture, which was the least of his pains.

Indeed, here was suffering far beyond anything the human mind can grasp, not only in terms of *extent*, but in terms of profound paradoxes. The perfect person suffered as though guilty. The Judge of all the Earth received the heaviest conceivable stroke of justice. The Great Physician suffered unparalleled affliction. The Creator of the universe died. Calvary was truly an event far beyond the evaluation and measurement of watching eyes, hymnwriter Joseph Swain describing this aspect of Christ's passion in these verses:–

> *They pierced through his hands and his feet,*
>   *His body he freely resigned;*
> *The pains of his flesh were so great!*
>   *But greater the pangs of his mind!*

> *Such wrath as would kindle a hell*
>   *Of never-abating despair*
> *For millions of sinners – then fell*
>   *On Jesus, and spent itself there.*

> *No nearer we venture to gaze*
>   *On sorrow so deep, so profound;*
> *But tread with amazement, and praise,*
>   *And reverence such hallowed ground.*

3. Christ's Desolation Indicated

To focus on the chief element of Christ's atonement, the hours of darkness also convey something of the unique mental anguish suffered by the Lord through his experience of separation from the Father. It was this terrible sensation that led to the cry, as the darkness came to an end, 'My God, my God, why hast thou forsaken me?' The deep gloom signified his aloneness and sense of abandonment which took the form of a crushing grief, a vacuum of hope, and a sense of eternal banishment. Christian people can never appreciate enough the comprehensive nature of the agonies of Christ as he took upon himself the very feelings that they deserve to suffer. It is beyond the compass of the human mind, especially when it is remembered that he bore the compounded desolation of many millions.

It is true that in his *divine nature* Christ could never be cut off from the Father, but whatever pain he suffered in his *human nature* would be equally *felt* in his divine being, because the two natures of Christ are truly indivisible. Thus, in his total being he was compelled to suffer *all* for us, and taste the unspeakable experience of having the door of hope, Heaven, and happiness slammed shut, leaving him in a dark and terrible abyss.

All our sin, and the love of it – including the sins of pride, unbelief and wilful rejection of mercy – deserve the righteous anger and indignation of God's justice, and Christ suffered the full consequences of being under that wrath. The hours of darkness speak of the appalling extent of despair borne by our representative and sinbearer in his amazing love and mercy for sinners.

4. Believers Called to See their Sin at Calvary

The hours of obscured vision bring into mental view the very heart of Calvary, calling people to see themselves there with Christ, who suffered not for himself, but for them. In a real sense we were there, as he bore *our* sins, not his own. All *our* evil deeds, words and thoughts were put on the sinless Saviour and purged away.

If we were to contemplate Calvary, visualising and imagining our Lord's tortured features, our sympathies would be so exercised that we would have no capacity to realise that *our sins* were on him. The hours of darkness seem to tell us not to visualise only the suffering person of Christ, but to see that our sins afflicted him. An old Reformation hymn expresses this with great feeling:–

> Extended on a cursèd tree,
>   Besmeared with dust, and sweat, and blood,
> See there, the King of glory see!
>   Sinks and expires the Son of God.
>
> Who, who, my Saviour, this has done?
>   Who would thy sacred body wound?
> No guilt thy spotless heart has known,
>   No guile has in thy lips been found.
>
> I, I alone, have done the deed!
>   'Tis I thy sacred flesh have torn;
> My sins have caused thee, Lord, to bleed,
>   Pointed the nail, and fixed the thorn.
>
> Too much to thee I cannot give;
>   Too much I cannot do for thee;
> Let all thy love, and all thy grief,
>   Grav'n on my heart for ever be!

When we consider Calvary, we should see, not a spectacle of execution, but a mighty transaction taking place, Christ dying for us – 'For he hath made him to be sin for us, who knew no sin.'[2] We should think, 'My pride was there; my greed; my self-seeking; and so many other sins committed day by day over so many years; including sins against light and truth.' No painting of Calvary and no movie can picture the reality of that event – that our sin was there.

5. The End of Spiritual Darkness Signified

The three hours of darkness were suddenly and decisively ended at the word of Christ (quoting the opening words of *Psalm 22*), 'Eli, Eli, lama sabachthani . . . My God, my God, why hast thou forsaken me?'[3] Soon afterwards he declared, 'It is finished . . . Father, into thy hands I commend my spirit,'[4] and his sacred body surrendered the flame of life.

> *'Twas justice that fell in that hour*
> *On Jesus our Saviour's dear head;*
> *Divinity's indwelling power*
> *Sustained him till nature was dead.*

Had there been no darkness, there could not have been a dramatic end of darkness, but this was a fitting way of picturing the successful end of the Lord's atoning work. As this concluded, darkness was vanquished, and so it was for Christ's saved people. That was the moment when the darkness of their condemnation was ended, and the deep gloom of their lost spiritual state was taken away. By the return of light, nature celebrated the accomplishments of Christ's death.

Only the words of Christ could dismiss the darkness, both then and now. Man's feeble lamps of learning, philosophy, art, poetry or psychology will never explain or resolve the sinful condition of

---

2 *2 Corinthians 5.21*
3 *Matthew 27.46*
4 *John 19.30*

the human race, because only Christ's words can do so. Only the Saviour's atonement could satisfy the demands and the righteous anger of the holy God towards sin.

The question addressed by Christ to his Father, 'Why hast thou forsaken me?' was asked not for his own benefit, for he knew all things, but for ours. To the bystanders the words of *Psalm 22* were Messianic, speaking of a coming suffering Saviour, and when Christ quoted from that psalm he announced that he was the Messiah, and that he had finished the work of atonement. His self-identification marked the climax of his agonies. Only Christ could atone, and only he could terminate the profound darkness surrounding the greatest benevolent act of all human history.

6. A Sign that All is Received by Faith

Half the passion of Christ took place under cover of darkness as a reminder and a warning that Christ cannot be sought by *sight*, but only by *faith*. No one can be truly converted by gazing at a crucifix, or by meditating on a mental picture of his ordeal. Divine grace cannot be received by viewing the stations of the cross, or by any form of sustained visualising of the physical features of his death.

We can only faintly imagine the physical aspects of Calvary, and although they move us and stir our indebtedness and love to Christ, we are saved not by contemplating *them*, but by resting our faith on the invisible accomplishments of our suffering Saviour. We hold our gaze not on Christ's physical agonies, even less on movies depicting exclusively the physical aspect, but we look with the eye of faith at the compassion, love and mercy of the incarnate God, and at the greatest accomplishment ever – the purchase of eternal souls. We say with Isaac Watts:–

> *See from his head, his hands, his feet,*
> *Sorrow and love flow mingling down:*
> *Did e'er such love and sorrow meet*
> *Or thorns compose so rich a crown?*

The dark hours of Calvary caution us on this matter, and send believers to Calvary by the route of faith.

7. The Work of Salvation Concealed from Scornful Minds

Second to the cross, the most prominent feature of Calvary was the shouted insults of onlookers. 'Let him save himself,' taunted rulers and common people alike. 'If thou be the Son of God, come down from the cross.'[5] 'He saved others; himself he cannot save.' 'He trusted in God; let him deliver him now.'[6] But as soon as thick darkness enveloped the scene, all ridicule was immediately silenced. How could they shout their cynical derision when filled with fear and confusion, unable to see what was happening at the place of crucifixion? Perhaps, under cover of darkness, sympathisers were removing Christ from the cross. Perhaps the Father had transported him away like Elijah. There was neither sun nor moon, and people did not carry lamps in broad daylight, so who could be sure what was happening? Many in that great crowd recalled famous prophecies in the books of *Isaiah, Joel* and *Micah* which spoke of a dramatic failing of sun, moon and stars, with divine punishment upon the land.[7]

The mocking crowd had yelled abuse for three hours; now they would see nothing, signifying how God would also blind the minds of cynics and slanderers throughout time so that Christ's sacred transaction for sinners would be beyond their grasp and reach.[8] Scornful unbelievers will never be allowed to see the hidden depths of the atonement, nor understand the reasons for the Lord's torment. There can be no realisation of redemption unless at the same time pride and unbelief fall. This truth is surely part of the intended

---

5   *Matthew 27.40*
6   *Matthew 27.43*
7   For example: *Isaiah 13.10; Joel 3.15; Micah 3.6*
8   *2 Corinthians 4.4*

message of the hours of darkness. When the mercy of God is about to open a person's spiritually blind eyes in conversion, he first prepares the way by removing that person's contempt for Christ. But for all who remain implacably opposed or indifferent to Christ, disdaining salvation or presuming themselves too good to need a Saviour, a pall of darkness will obscure the meaning and power of Calvary, and all hope of salvation.

As for the people who watched the Lord suffer, they had sinned against the prophets by their unbelief, and against Christ despite his miracles, character and teaching. Now they would see nothing until the Spirit came down on the Day of Pentecost to pierce many hearts, and bring them to repentance.

8. Activity of the Hosts of Darkness Indicated

When the chief priests, elders and captains of the Temple came to arrest the Lord, he said to them, 'This is your hour, and the power of darkness.'[9] We believe the hour of the power of darkness refers not only to Christ's taking divine wrath for sinners, but also to the mysterious onslaught of Satan and his demons upon the Lord as he hung on Calvary's cross. The three dark hours fittingly suggest their terrible activity.

In referring to this we stress again that the principal and most important way in which Christ conquered the devil and his legions was that he bore the punishment due to believers for all the sins which stood against them. By doing this he set them free from eternal punishment, and thwarted Satan's design to bring them down to hell. Satan was defeated because he no longer had any claim to those people for whom Christ died.[10]

However, Satan's desperate unleashing of rage and spite toward Christ as he suffered on the cross must not be overlooked. Filled

9   *Luke 22.53*
10 *Revelation 12.10*

with fury, the demons of darkness hemmed the Saviour round in a vicious if hopeless endeavour to divert him from his atoning objectives, possibly even by bringing him into sin. At Calvary they unleashed upon him all the hatred they possessed, for although they sensed that their hour of defeat had come, blind rage gave rise to a desperate, optimistic vindictiveness. C. H. Spurgeon once described this element of Calvary in these words:

'The howlings of hell rise in awful clamour. The pit is emptying out its legions. Terrible as lions, hungry as wolves, and black as night, the demons rush on in myriads.'

Who can tell what horrors Christ bore in the hour of 'the power of darkness'? But at the end he was shown to be victorious over them all, and 'led captivity captive'.[11] Then, 'having spoiled principalities and powers, he made a shew of them openly, triumphing over them in it'.[12]

Christ as Saviour took the literal and eternal punishment of our sin, bore its consequences entirely, and also suffered the venomous onslaught of devils who could not endure the thought of captive sinners gaining liberty. Edward Henry Bickersteth enshrined this aspect of Messiah's victory in noble verse, picturing the moment of the Lord's death and the journey of his soul to Heaven:–

> *Around his disembodied soul the powers*
> *Of darkness swarm'd, and Satan face to face*
> *With burning falchion barr'd his path. One look,*
> *Mere virtue bent on mere maliciousness,*
> *Pierced him like lightning, and shot withering fire*
> *Among his blasted hosts. Distraught they stood,*
> *Insensible, one moment; and then fell*
> *From round him, as the billow's cloven pride*
> *Falls in thick spray from off the vessel's prow . . .*
>
> (Yesterday, Today and Forever)

Until the day dawns when we enter Paradise we will never grasp

11 *Ephesians 4.8*
12 *Colossians 2.15*

more than a tiny part of the cost of our redemption, and how greatly Christ has loved us. McCheyne's famous lines say –

> *Then, Lord, shall I fully know*
> *Not till then, how much I owe.*

*   *   *

In focusing on the three hours of darkness we do not intend to give the impression that the agonies of atonement were confined to this period of time. We realise that Christ suffered the full anguish of atonement throughout six hours, and even before in the Garden of Gethsemane the very awareness of what lay before him was crushing beyond human endurance. But the reasons for the time of darkness must surely serve to concentrate understanding of the price paid for human redemption.

No doubt more matters than those mentioned in these pages were signified by the dark hours of Calvary. Surely they were a call to all those present, and to us also, to *think*. They took away sight so that people would reflect on the meaning of the death of a mighty miracle worker identified by many as the expected Messiah. The long wait in that darkness summoned the people to remember the suffering servant of *Isaiah 53*, to probe their hearts, to look within, and to make a repentant response to God.

It is also likely that the dark hours were prophetic, speaking of the treatment that would be meted out to the Christ of Calvary throughout the remainder of human history as 'works' religions sought to obscure his work, and as atheism fought to suppress it.

Certainly, those dark hours were full of meaning, because with Christ, even the darkness has light for the soul. We borrow the words of David in *Psalm 139* and use them to describe the dark hours of Calvary: 'If I say, Surely the darkness shall cover me; even the night shall be light about me.'[13]

---

13 *Psalm 139.11*

From – *Yesterday, Today and Forever*

by Edward Henry Bickersteth, 1825-1906

Was love stronger than death? Upon that cross
They grappled as in final strife. For now
Hell put forth all its malice, and let loose
Its gather'd vengeance. All the air was dense
With fiends, and blackness, blacker than the night
Which Moses' rod on smitten Egypt drew,
Dismay'd the heavens: such delegated power
Had Satan, regent of the air, and all
The gloomy hosts of darkness at his beck
Hemming the Saviour round. And, as the load
Immense, intolerable, of the world's sin,
Casting its dreadful shadow high as Heaven,
Deep as Gehenna, nearer and more near
Grounded at last upon that Sinless Soul
With all its crushing weight and killing curse,
Then first, from all eternity then first,
From his beloved Son the Father's face
Was slowly averted, and its light eclipsed.

7
The New Birth

'Verily, verily, I say unto thee, Except a man be born again,
he cannot see the kingdom of God' *(John 3.3).*

THE TERM 'born again Christian' has been massively
devalued in recent years, having been freely misapplied by
the media. Stripped of its true meaning, this description is
also claimed by a variety of well-known worldly personalities, many
of whom admit they hardly ever attend church.

Being 'born again' is also a favourite term with happy-clappy
style Christians, many of whom lack any depth of commitment to
their Christianity. Yet it is a vital concept which should never have
been cheapened, for it was introduced by Christ with the weighty
words, 'Verily, verily' (the double amen). Today we would say, 'I most
solemnly assure you . . .'

The new birth was first mentioned when a leading Jewish teacher
went to Christ late one evening, most probably to open negotiations
with the Lord to secure his cooperation with the Temple authorities
in Jerusalem. The very first words of the narrative (in *John's Gospel*)

set the scene: 'There was a man of the Pharisees, named Nicodemus.'[1] The most important feature of this man was not his name, but the fact that he was a Pharisee. The Gospel writer seems to say, 'There was a Pharisee, who, incidentally, was named Nicodemus.' This is significant because the need for new birth was about to be urged upon a prominent religious teacher who was clearly a member of the supreme Jewish council, the Sanhedrin. We learn from this that people who are very religious are not necessarily true believers in the eyes of Christ, and may need to be altogether changed before they can enter Christ's kingdom.

What factors would disqualify a Pharisee from being a true member of the kingdom? Why should Christ have regarded them as spiritually blind when they believed many right doctrines? They honoured the Old Testament Scriptures, and unlike the other main religious 'party' of those days, the Sadducees, they believed in the immortality of the soul and the coming day of judgement. Their great mistake, however, was their belief that God accepted people on the basis of personal merit.

To begin with, there was the merit of being Jewish, which in their view secured immediate favour from God. In addition, Pharisees believed that if they meticulously kept the ceremonial aspects of the system of worship given to them by God, they would earn even greater favour and the very best places in Heaven. To make matters more complicated numerous extra rules had been added to those given in Scripture, and all these the Pharisees scrupulously kept, with ever-growing self-satisfaction at their prowess. Religion for them was all tied up with external rites, but there was little attention to the sinful state of the heart, and no desire to know and relate to God in a personal way.

All this was true of Nicodemus, who was not a priest, but a scribe or interpreter of Scripture. He may have been the most respected

---

1   *John 3.1*

of all Jewish teachers at that time, because the Lord called him 'the teacher'.[2] Yet even such a teacher needed to be born again.

To some extent there is a Pharisee in most of us. If we like the idea of having a religion, we prefer one that involves no personal contact with God. Also, our preference is for a God whose favour can be earned, giving us something to be proud of. Many people recoil when they hear that the message of Christ offers free salvation to repentant sinners, objecting that it requires them to grovel and acknowledge their wrongdoing. The Pharisee within does not want to approach God as a humble supplicant.

Christ and Nicodemus taught exactly opposite ways to relate to God, the Lord presenting *grace* as the only way of salvation, and Nicodemus insisting on *works*. In other words the conflicting routes to Heaven were, on the one hand, free pardon for repentant sinners, and on the other, acceptance with God by one's own achievements. Why did Nicodemus approach the miracle-working teacher of grace, when he held the opposite position?

Most probably, as we have said, it was to open discussions on some kind of pact. The Pharisees and Temple clergy were losing the hearts of the people, who were becoming more interested in Christ. The Lord, by his miracles and his compelling teaching, was stealing their thunder and causing them to be sidelined. Could Jesus, Nicodemus wondered, be accommodated and absorbed by the religious establishment?

For four centuries the Jews had not seen a wonder-working prophet. What lustre such a prophet would add to the priests and scribes if Christ could be adopted by them! Such an arrangement would not be easy, because the Saviour's teachings would have to be toned down to agree with theirs, and he would have to stop saying he was the Son of God, but surely he would value their recognition,

---

2   *John 3.10* is translated in the *KJV,* 'Art thou a master of Israel?' but strictly the article should be '*the* master', and 'master' means teacher.

and the security and rewards that would come to him.

The conversation opened with the Pharisee voicing his diplomatic acknowledgement that Jesus must be from God to work such miracles. He could hardly say anything less because many miracles had been performed in Jerusalem that very week, and we know from the Gospel narratives that the Lord's healings were always radical, instantaneous, irreversible, and mostly were performed under full public scrutiny. However, the proud heart of Nicodemus did not for a moment accept that Christ was the Messiah.

Nicodemus was only halfway through his opening sentence when the hoped-for negotiations were terminated by Christ's famous words – 'Verily, verily, I say unto thee, Except a man be born again, he cannot see the kingdom of God.'[3]

The obvious implication was that Nicodemus, for all his reputation as a teacher, knew nothing and could see nothing spiritually because he needed to experience a total change of heart and life. Christ was answering the question that the Pharisee should have asked, namely: 'How can a person be accepted by God?' The Lord's words – 'Verily, verily' made his statement dogmatic and inflexible, allowing no exceptions. To see, taste and experience God, everyone must be born again.

Dogmatic statements are not acceptable in today's culture, but everyone realises that sometimes they are necessary. Who would want a surgeon who watered down the urgency of essential surgery and made it sound no more necessary than self-treatment with dandelion tea? If we want to be told the truth about physical matters, how much more should we want plain language where Heaven or hell are involved?

Christ said, in effect, there is only one way to spiritual life and Heaven, and that is by a new birth, or as the original Greek says, a birth from above. This birth analogy provides some startling insights

3   *John 3.3*

into the nature of Christian conversion. For example, a baby does not bring about his own birth using his brains and so making his way into the world. Birth is a process outside his power, and spiritual new birth exactly parallels this. An unbeliever is brought to see his need of Christ's pardon and renewing grace. He sincerely believes in Christ, repents of his sin and prays for spiritual life, soon becoming aware that he has been altogether changed and brought into communion with the Lord. The great change is not wrought by the new believer, but by God.

Another parallel between physical and spiritual birth is that both usher an entirely new person into the world. In the case of a person who is born again, former sins no longer have mastery because a wholly new nature and outlook begin to operate in that person. Mean people become generous, violent people become gentle, selfish people become sensitive and helpful to others, hopeless liars are given a new integrity, and the chief sin of pride is dramatically diminished. So much is made new that Paul says, 'Therefore if any man be in Christ, he is a new creature: old things are passed away; behold, all things are become new.'[4]

Another parallel is seen in the fact that physical birth is generally dramatic and sudden, and so is the new birth. Certainly people may seek the Lord for some time if they delay repentance, or do not mean it sincerely. Some seekers are slow to yield their lives to Christ, or trust him alone for salvation. On this last point, some seekers mistakenly think that while Christ's atoning death is necessary for their forgiveness, yet their own record is good enough to merit some of the blessing. But Christ can only save a seeker who says (in the words of Toplady's hymn) –

> *Nothing in my hand I bring;*
> *Simply to thy Cross I cling.*

---

4   *2 Corinthians 5.17*

Once repentance and faith in Christ is sincere, and the seeker yields to him, the great change of the new birth may be consciously experienced, and all things made new. Conversion is not a lifelong process but a birth.

Conversion is illustrated by birth in yet another way, because birth leads to growth, nurturing and education before maturity is attained. Conversion is the same. Once born again, the believer is (i) on the road to Heaven, (ii) engaged in the battle for progressive ongoing personal holiness, and (iii) in the school of Christ for learning more of him. Spiritual birth produces a complete 'baby' Christian, but growth lies ahead.

Returning to Nicodemus, this eminent man was taken aback and wounded by the gentle bluntness of Christ's statement that he could know nothing of God without a new birth. His instant reaction was one of sarcasm: 'How can a man be born when he is old? can he enter the second time into his mother's womb, and be born?'[5]

As a leading interpreter Nicodemus was a highly intelligent man, and would have known perfectly well that the Lord's mention of new birth was a metaphor, telling him he needed radical and spiritual transformation. But to express his scorn he returned the same metaphor with a twist, saying, in effect, 'How can you expect a mature teacher like me to start all over again? In normal life no eminent teacher is made to go back to the nursery class. Your words are offensive and unreasonable.' And this is precisely the reaction that so many of us had when first confronted with the Gospel of grace.

Christ, however, replied by reinforcing his point with another illustration from childbirth: 'Verily, verily, I say unto thee, Except a man be born of water and of the Spirit, he cannot enter into the kingdom of God. That which is born of the flesh is flesh; and that which is born of the Spirit is spirit.'[6]

---

5   John 3.4
6   John 3.5-6

'Born of water' refers to the breaking of a mother's waters at the beginning of labour, and the Lord used this to picture physical birth. However, there is no spiritual life or communion with God until the person is also born of the Spirit of God. The person born of the flesh is only flesh, and the birth to spiritual life needs to take place. To have only physical birth is to be a true human being, but one cut off from God and lacking spiritual life and faculties. Only the Holy Spirit can give these things in the new birth.

'Do not regard this as all too astonishing,' said the Lord to Nicodemus. 'It is imperative; you must be born again.' Interestingly the 'you' in these words of Christ is a plural 'you', as though he said, 'All you Pharisees must be born again.' Even religious teachers and ministers may not have sought or found the new birth.

Despite the similarities between childbirth and spiritual birth, there is a marked difference in the way they are achieved, this difference being described by the Lord in these words:–

'The wind bloweth where it listeth, and thou hearest the sound thereof, but canst not tell whence it cometh, and whither it goeth: so is every one that is born of the Spirit.'[7]

While childbirth is a highly visible event involving a midwife and perhaps other helpers, spiritual birth is an inner secret work of the Holy Spirit. It is not imparted by any rite or ceremony by a church, but by the marvellous power of God.

However, like the power of an invisible gale, the effects of the Spirit's work are very apparent. To add to the kind of changes already mentioned, by conversion the pliable person becomes strong, the coarse and immoral person becomes refined, the naive person becomes discerning, the fearful one becomes courageous, and the sullen individual becomes happy and content. Every convert receives a new mind, a new way of thinking, and new attitudes and tastes.

The Christian church has always seen magnificent examples of

7   John 3.8

transformation in people who come to Christ, changes that could not be accomplished any other way than by new birth by the power of the Holy Spirit. When people are converted, their relations and work colleagues or fellow students are usually surprised at the difference in them.

As his encounter with Christ moved to a climax, Nicodemus still resisted Christ's words, exclaiming, 'How can these things be?' His complaint seemed to encompass several grounds for protest. 'How can these things be so,' he seems to say, 'when a renowned teacher like myself has never heard of them? This is contrary to all I have ever thought. To believe and submit to this, my entire life would have to change and I would have to become nothing at all. Besides all this, a simple and uneducated person could have this new birth, and be on the same level as I. How can such things be?'

Nicodemus also appeared to be asking, 'And why should such a conversion be necessary at all?' The answer to that is that the holiness of God requires it. No work or attainments of ours can satisfy God or make up for our long record of sin. Salvation must be a gift of grace secured by the atoning work of the Saviour, and it must involve the re-making of a person by God.

Sadly, Christ was compelled to say to Nicodemus that he, in common with his fellow leaders, did not embrace his message. The noted Pharisee would not accept his need of Christ, or yield his life to him. There is every hope that he did so later, because *John's Gospel* records how he defended Christ in the Sanhedrin, and subsequently contributed to his burial costs.[8]

In the final part of the Lord's meeting with Nicodemus he gave important warnings coupled with what is probably the best-known verse in the Bible about the love of God. Addressing the eminent teacher, Christ first said: 'If I have told you earthly things, and ye

8 *John 7.50-52; 19.39-42*

believe not, how shall ye believe, if I tell you of heavenly things?'[9]

In essence the Lord said, 'I have told you about spiritual new birth, an experience which takes place here on Earth, but which determines your heavenly future. I have also illustrated conversion using understandable earthly metaphors. If you do not believe these things, you will never be able to grasp or appreciate the deep things of God.' In other words, without conversion the renowned interpreter would know nothing.

Next there came from the lips of Christ a picture of his death, when he would be lifted up on Calvary's cross to gain eternal life for believers. Then came the tremendous words – 'For God so loved the world, that he gave his only begotten Son, that whosoever believeth in him should not perish, but have everlasting life.'[10]

Believing is everything. The benefits of Christ's atoning death come only to those who truly believe in him. They believe in what he did as the essential and only way to be forgiven. They believe in everything he said, including the terms of salvation: sincere repentance, faith, and submission to his direction in life. Believing is the only key to the door of the eternal kingdom.

Nicodemus received a closing, searching warning in these words: 'And this is the condemnation, that light is come into the world, and men loved darkness rather than light, because their deeds were evil.'[11] Would the Pharisee reject the call of Christ to seek the new birth on intellectual grounds? Would his past training make it impossible for him to believe? The Lord's reply indicated that no person refuses the light of the Gospel on account of intellectual doubts. The problem is never in the head, but always in the heart. If Nicodemus turned away from the light of Christ, it would be because he loved his own sinful, self-serving objectives more. In his case, this meant he would

---

9   *John 3.12*
10 *John 3.16*
11 *John 3.19;* the interview with Nicodemus continues to the end of verse 21.

value his pharisaical pride in himself, his reputation and position in society, and his inner sin more than forgiveness and new life from Christ. This would be the real cause of his rejection of the Saviour's love. The same is true of everyone – that unbelief really emanates from the heart and not the mind.

Nicodemus probably changed his attitude as time went by, seeing his need of pardon and new life, and realising that Jesus was truly the Messiah. Christ's discourse on the new birth would have been, at first, offensive to him, but later he would have seen the necessity of it, and the divine kindness and power in it. 'Ye must be born again,' rang in that Pharisee's ears until it overwhelmed his heart.

An almost parallel statement of Christ, made to his disciples, powerfully confirms that a new life is essential to authentic Christianity:– 'Verily I say unto you, Except ye be converted, and become as little children, ye shall not enter into the kingdom of heaven.'[12]

The new birth, as every believer has proved, ushers in a life of fellowship with God, answered prayer, guidance, help, peace, learning of him and anticipation of eternal glory. The Christian faith teaches that death instantly transfers the soul of the believer to the paradise of Christ, waiting for the end of Earth's present history and the day of the resurrection of the body when –

> *My new-created form shall rise;*
> *Adapted for the Earth and skies;*
> *A body earthly, yet sublime,*
> *Above restraints of flesh and time.*

We turn next to the topic of the resurrection of Christ, the key to the personal resurrection of all who trust in him, at that last day.

---

12 *Matthew 18.3*

8

Why the Resurrection?

What the Resurrection Was Designed to Achieve

'Why seek ye the living among the dead?
He is not here, but is risen' *(Luke 24.5-6).*

EVEN AMONG CHRISTIANS, many people do not really know why the resurrection of Christ took place. They think that it was solely intended as a miracle to prove that Christ was God. It certainly convinced the disciples and many others who saw the risen Lord, but two thousand years later it is not very useful for persuading cynics about Christ, because they have not seen it for themselves. They say that it only happened according to very old literature, and this is hardly proof for today.

The resurrection, however, did not take place in order to give irrefutable proof to *cynics* in later ages, but to teach and assure *believers* of a number of vital matters, eight of which are presented in this chapter. Christ rose from the dead and appeared to his disciples over a period of forty days before ascending into Heaven so that Christian believers may learn and cherish the following great truths.

1. The Success of Calvary

The first purpose of Christ's resurrection was to demonstrate the total success of the atonement, because if Christ had not risen and openly appeared to the disciples, no one would ever be certain that the punishment of sin had been fully borne before he gave up the spirit and died. But by the power of his divine nature he rose again, showing that a complete atonement had been made for his people.

Paul writes that Christ 'was delivered for our offences, and was raised again for our justification,'[1] meaning that his well-attested resurrection signalled the complete success of his atoning work, and its sufficiency in securing our acceptance with God.

Christ's resurrection also proves that his offering of righteousness to earn Heaven for all believers was perfect, and accepted by the Father. Christ's resurrection, followed in due course by his ascension to Heaven, could never have taken place if he had failed. Being God incarnate, Christ could never have failed. However, he did not leave believers wondering and open to doubt, but rose and appeared physically, visibly, audibly and unmistakably to proclaim and confirm the completion of his redemptive work. This gives assurance to believers rather than tangible proof to cynics.

2. The Lord's Power Over Death

In *John 2.19* it is recorded that Christ said – 'Destroy this temple, and in three days I will raise it up.' The record goes on to explain that he spoke of the 'temple of his body'.

In *John 10.17-18* the Lord said: 'Therefore doth my Father love me, because I lay down my life, that I might take it again. No man taketh it from me, but I lay it down of myself. I have power to lay it down, and I have power to take it again. This commandment have I received of my Father.'

---

1   *Romans 4.25*

Such verses confirm Christ's power to bring about his own resurrection, and also explain the apparent discrepancy between different scriptures on this point, because some seem to attribute the resurrection to the Father, such as *Acts 2.24* and *32* which includes the phrase – 'This Jesus hath God raised up.' When the Lord said: 'This commandment have I received of my Father,' he showed that the Father sanctioned, authorised and approved the resurrection of the Son. Expressed in human terms, the Father looked upon the suffering and death of his Son, and affirmed that he had wholly borne the punishment due to his people, perfectly fulfilling all that was necessary for their redemption. So the Father gave commandment and sanction to the Son for the resurrection.

The Son was raised up by his own power, while the Father shared by giving the fullest authorisation. Christ, while he was acting as our representative, lived as an obedient Son who did only what the Father authorised.

Why is it so important to see that Christ rose from the dead by his own power? Because this act showed that he is 'the resurrection, and the life', and the prince of life, who is able to bring believers through death, and ultimately raise their bodies also. Christ demonstrated that he possessed within himself the power to break the historic bondage of death.

Why is it important to see that the Father was involved also? Because the approval of the Father proves that Christ's offering was perfect, and that he was fully entitled to rise to assume glorified human form and the lordship of his people. Christ was the appointed Saviour, the qualified Saviour, and in the resurrection, the accredited Saviour.

3. Christ's Headship of the Church Revealed

Another reason why the Lord did not ascend into glory in a spiritual and invisible way is explained in *Romans 1.4*, where Paul says that by resurrection Christ was – 'declared to be the Son of God with power'. *Declared* means that Christ was marked out and publicly appointed. In other words, at the resurrection he was shown to have re-assumed his full power and lordship as the Son of God. He was also proclaimed as having kept a human body which he would wear eternally as Lord of his ransomed people.

What greater assurance could there be of Christ's special interest in us than that he should display his risen body before ascending into Heaven, showing that he would wear human nature throughout eternity? What more could he have done to convince his people that he would rule and care for them, making them his special concern and delight? His revealing of his risen power was the ultimate proof that he had pledged himself to his redeemed people, and would never leave them nor forsake them.

The resurrection declares in a resounding way the Lord's assumption of the final and everlasting stage of kingship over his people – 'For to this end Christ both died, and rose, and revived, that he might be Lord both of the dead and living.'[2]

4. The Future of Believers Revealed

The resurrection also has the purpose of encouraging the faith of believers in their own eventual bodily resurrection, and showing what that body will be like. In *Romans 8.11* Paul says, 'But if the Spirit of him that raised up Jesus from the dead dwell in you, he that raised up Christ from the dead shall also quicken your mortal bodies by his Spirit that dwelleth in you.' The Lord had previously promised that he would rise again so that his disciples might be assured of their future resurrection, saying, 'Because I live, ye shall live also.'[3]

Further details are given in *1 Corinthians 15.20:* 'But now is Christ risen from the dead, and become the firstfruits of them that slept.' It was fitting that the practical results of Christ's work should be

---

2   *Romans 14.9*
3   *John 14.19*

revealed first in himself, as Forerunner. The resurrection shows that when, in the last day of this present Earth, the bodies of believers are raised, reconstituted, and rejoined with their souls, these new bodies will not be the same as they were before death. In this life our bodies are 'of the earth, *earthy*', but on resurrection day they will be *heavenly, incorruptible*, and altogether changed.[4]

When Christ rose from the dead, it was obvious to the disciples that he had changed physically. His previous body had not merely been resuscitated so that he could return to the same kind of life as before. Previously the physical body of the Lord had been weak, subject to fatigue and pain, and capable of dying, but after he broke the bands of death and returned to life, the physical aspects of his humanity were vastly higher and more glorious than before.

After the resurrection Christ's body was endowed with new qualities, possessing energies and capabilities not previously seen. He would suddenly appear in the midst of the disciples, though the doors of the room were locked. Yet he was touchable and tangible, and able to eat with his disciples. He would vanish from their sight mysteriously, and, at his ascension, defy gravity, rising serenely from Earth to Heaven.

All this was intended to show that the risen Lord had brought about a new humanity for the occupation of the eternal realm. Had Christ not risen, such wonders would never have been seen, and could not have been easily understood and appreciated. From the resurrection of Christ we are assured of the details of our eternal future. From the time of resurrection, we shall wear glorified bodies adapted for the eternal state. These will be visible, recognisable and touchable, but incapable of deterioration and decay, of sickness or tiredness. Then we shall be perfectly suited to the eternal city of God, when a rebuilt Earth shall have been made heavenly, and Heaven shall have come down to Earth.

---

4   *1 Corinthians 15.47-52*

5. The Lord's Triumph Over Satan Manifested

The resurrection of Christ was essential to validate a harrowing yet unseen aspect of the work of Christ, that is, his victory over Satan, his objectives and all that he represents. He had to be *seen* to be the victor in the greatest battle of history. It is important to know that the death of the Lord, while primarily a matter of atonement, was also a demonstration of the superiority of good over evil, of godliness over rebellion, and of God over Satan. In his perfect life Christ vindicated the standards of God, showing that righteousness was feasible and wonderful, and in his obedience unto death he showed the beauty of mercy and kindness, by contrast with the lies and cruelty of Satan.

The psalmist David caught the spirit of this aspect of Calvary and the resurrection, saying, 'Let God arise, let his enemies be scattered . . . Thou hast ascended on high, thou hast led captivity captive: thou hast received gifts for men; yea, for the rebellious also, that the Lord God might dwell among them.'[5] In *Ephesians 4*, the words of this psalm are shown to refer to the risen Saviour, leading a host of captives at his ascension. His resurrection is seen as the demonstration of a mighty victory.

Consider the case of Satan, a privileged and glorious angel who fell through pride, becoming an evil rebel, and doing his utmost to bring down the human race in order to make Christ's creation of a peopled world a failure. If he should get away with this, it would prove that rebellion against God is stronger than obedience, that wickedness pays, and that evil will prevail over purity.

Must the world wait until the day of judgement to see any vindication of the superiority of holiness over wickedness and rebellion? No, because the resurrection constitutes a visible victory of Christ over Satan.

It is true that in this world we continually observe apparent

---

5   *Psalm 68.1, 18*

victories of evil over good through crime and oppression, and every other abuse of God's standards, and it would appear that it pays to be crooked, greedy, proud and dishonest. But the perfect man came to Earth to reveal the glories of righteousness, and to put to shame the evil of spiritual rebellion. As the representative of the human race, and also as the representative of lovingkindness, mercy and truth, Christ went to Calvary both to save and to demonstrate his own ultimate power.

Who would prevail on that cross? Would the perfect representative man survive temptation, persecution, reviling, then death by crucifixion? Or would Satan, bent on causing Christ's destruction or withdrawal, end the mission of salvation? The resurrection signalled that righteousness had prevailed, and tenderness and faithfulness had triumphed. Christ surmounted all and had the victory. Satan would no longer be able to lay claim to billions of people who would look to Christ for salvation. With Satan's claims broken, the human race (represented by believers) would revive, and in due course judgement would fall on Satan.

Cowering in the shadows around Calvary was a defeated Satan with his demonic hosts, and the personification of pride, selfishness, violence and deceit shrank away in the presence of the perfect man.

In every age and in every culture a decisive military victory has been marked with due ceremony by a formal taking of surrender, together with the imposition of terms, and a victory parade. *Psalm 68* uses the picture of the ancient conquering king who, having vanquished his enemies, marches into his new possession. And by this picture, the psalm looks forward to the conquest achieved by Christ and celebrated by the resurrection.

Edward Henry Bickersteth, in the Victorian epic poem, *Yesterday, Today and Forever* referred to earlier, pictures Christ at his resurrection and ascension as a great vessel sailing through the sea, the demons of darkness being cast from the prow and hurled to either side to form a long, captive wake at the rear.

The resurrection of Christ demonstrates the superiority of the Saviour over Satan, a dependant and rebellious created spirit. Resurrection is the triumph of God's authority over self-determination and disobedience. It is the triumph of infinite wisdom over mere created intelligence. It is the triumph of the Lord of liberty over the serpent who brought in slavery to sin and death.

There most certainly had to be a resurrection to mark the multifaceted victory of Christ. The resurrection is that most momentous of victory parades – a manifestation of the triumph of Christ, the embodiment of every precious virtue, over all that is base. Conquest is a key word in the appreciation of the resurrection.

6. Christ Commended as Lord

The resurrection completes the commending of Christ to believers as their Lord for life and eternity.

The question may be asked – What entitlement and qualification does Christ have for the kingship of converted people? We may answer that he is their rightful King simply by virtue of being divine. He is in a sense their supreme monarch 'by birth'. He is also their rightful King by virtue of ownership, having exerted his creative power to bring all things into existence.

He is also qualified to be King by virtue of his attributes, which are infinitely superior to all the powers and capabilities of Satan and all human leaders put together. His qualifications are endless, for he knows all things, and no power on Earth can obstruct his plans and purposes. He has the right to be King by every possible argument with the exception of one, that he is not an *elected* King as far as the rebellious human race is concerned. His rightful subjects have turned their backs upon him, challenging his right to rule over them. They have made themselves loathsome and objectionable in his sight, abusing his standards, placing themselves under condemnation, shutting themselves out of his kingdom, and selling themselves into the bondage of Satan, who has become their lord.

By what process is Christ 'elected' by believers? Through his aton-ing death and righteous life Christ pays the price of sin and earns Heaven for his people. He is then seen as successful and triumphant in the resurrection, and through these things he becomes to believ-ers an overwhelmingly desirable Lord. Through his rising again he confirms salvation and people willingly look to him and choose him to be their everlasting King. The outcome is that by every conceiv-able argument and right, he reigns over them.

To crown and complete the work of atonement, there had to be a visible, earthly sight of the Saviour-King. As a bride chooses to marry her groom, so the church embraces Christ having seen him in his risen glory, and he is then King, not only by right, by creation, by qualifications, by purchase, and by conquest, but also by uninhibited free choice. It is by the resurrection that he is presented to us in all his regal authority, desirability and power.

7. The Divine Attributes Revealed in Christ

The resurrection was both inevitable and essential if the divine attributes were to be more fully seen in Christ before his entry into Heaven. It was highly appropriate that there should be a *complete* manifestation of Jesus Christ as God, for we read in *Colossians 2.9* that 'in him dwelleth all the fulness of the Godhead bodily'.

If we had only the Gospel accounts of the earthly life of Christ up to his death on Calvary, the full extent of his glory would not be seen, because his earthly walk showed the fatigue, weakness and death of his humiliation. It is true that in the events of his humiliation we see wonderful divine attributes manifested, such as his mercy and love, together with his holiness, wisdom and faithfulness, and many manifestations of power. But we do not see his power of *endless life*, his *unchangeability* or his *supreme invincibility*. The Cross is all humiliation, even in its display of divine attributes. The resurrection completes the picture.

Can God die? Could God fail? Would Christ be overpowered? The answer is obviously no, but only the resurrection fully demonstrates this answer.

In his resurrection the Saviour is proved right in everything he said and did. He is held up to view as the *infallible* Christ, and vindicated in his words, policy, and deeds. The resurrection justifies his *divine wisdom, foreknowledge* and *power* in ever submitting to Calvary. Though he was arrested in apparent weakness, and died in seemingly terminal agonies, the resurrection demonstrates that he knew exactly what he was doing, and that he fully succeeded in all his objectives.

The resurrection shows his *unchanging nature* because, although his bodily form is made altogether more glorious, yet he remains in every respect the same person and the same Lord. Even the *omnipresence* of his divine being is reflected in the events of the resurrection, because now he is able to appear to one or two in one place, and then to others elsewhere. The two disciples who arrived from the Emmaus road had no sooner told of how he was with them than suddenly he appears in the midst of all.

Great attributes of God are revealed in Christ, but the crowning picture is provided by his resurrection appearances.

8. Our Lord's Eternal Familiarity

A particularly heartening and reassuring purpose of the resurrection as far as believers are concerned is that it exhibits the unchanging and everlasting attitude of Christ toward those who love and trust him. Through his various post-resurrection appearances he showed his disciples that his manner towards them was entirely unaffected by his new, risen form, and that he would continue to be their familiar, personal friend and Lord even after his return to heavenly glory.

This purpose of the resurrection is seen in the appearance of Christ to the disciples recorded in *Luke 24.36*: 'And as they thus spake, Jesus himself stood in the midst of them, and saith unto them, Peace be unto you.' They were terrified, we read, and the Lord commended himself to them with immense kindness and priceless words:–

'And he said unto them, Why are ye troubled? and why do thoughts arise in your hearts? Behold my hands and my feet, that it is I myself: handle me, and see; for a spirit hath not flesh and bones, as ye see me have. And when he had thus spoken, he shewed them his hands and his feet. And while they yet believed not for joy, and wondered, he said unto them, Have ye here any meat? And they gave him a piece of a broiled fish, and of an honeycomb. And he took it, and did eat before them.'[6]

Then, just as he always had done, he taught them and 'opened their understanding'. He was clearly going to be their same friend and guide even after his ascent into Heaven.

People change, and the passing of the years causes many a shift in attitudes, affections and loyalties. Life's earliest and closest friends are often completely forgotten, and people who in youth were open, friendly and sympathetic, become cold, indifferent, and even hostile as time goes by. Some people achieve high things, becoming rich, influential and significant, and they cease to be the people they were, and have no time for the stock from which they came.

The early Christians may well have wondered whether the death of Christ and his return to his former heavenly station would change everything in his heart. Would he have a new remoteness? While on Earth, moving among his disciples, he related closely to them, show-ing them immense sympathy and affection. Once seated at the right hand of God, occupying his supreme place as the infinitely power-ful second person of the Trinity, and ruling with the Father and the Spirit, could those first believers be sure that he still possessed the close regard he had for them on Earth? Would the Christian idea of a caring, feelingful God die as an unrealistic romantic hope?

The resurrection gave them a sight of the risen Lord before he ascended. His humiliation was over, and his body beyond all further

6   *Luke 24.38-43*

harm. No band of Temple police or Roman soldiers could touch him now, and if they were to try, he would walk effortlessly through them. Would his attitude change also? Not at all, for they witnessed in the risen Lord the same kindness they had always known.

He appeared in remarkable power when the door was barred shut.[7] He was able to pass through walls and doors, and appear at will. These things alarmed them at first, but it was important that they should see him raised above the shackles and limitations of his former body. But he did not stand at a dignified distance or address them in a lofty, authoritative manner. He came gloriously, and yet in a most familiar manner, appearing among them, and exhibiting his continuing intimacy and friendship with them. Though he was Lord, nothing had changed. It was evident that in the future they would not be required to view him as a *remote* Sovereign, for he would remain as close to his people *spiritually* as when he had walked the dusty roads of the Holy Land with them.

In the resurrection he said he would be accessible always as their elder brother and their *friend*. 'I am eternally changed for you,' he seemed to say, 'yet I retain human nature, and shall wear it for ever for you. See in my body the scars of my sufferings, because here are the tokens and the evidence of my ongoing love for all my people. I appear to you as your risen Lord to show you that I am eternally yours, ever approachable, and always ready to share my presence, my love, my care, and my sustaining power with you.'

The resurrection is both deep and high in the magnificent scope of its purposes. It is the kindest imaginable communication from the Saviour to his people in every age. The very simple but message-rich meal of *Luke 24.41* says so much about the Lord's ongoing closeness to his people. They gave him a piece of broiled fish and of an honeycomb and he ate in their view, enacting the illustration or type for those times of fellowship and close relationship. He seems to be

---

7   *John 20.19*

saying to them, 'Just as I ate with you on Earth, so, as the resurrected Lord, I will always relate closely to you, and interact with you.'

9
Prophecies of Resurrection

*'Why should it be thought a thing incredible with you,
that God should raise the dead?' (Acts 26.8)*

THE WORDS QUOTED above were spoken by Paul (then a prisoner) to King Herod, who was well versed in the Old Testament. Paul meant that the king should have known that the Messiah would rise from the dead. Paul went further, telling the king that the theme of all his preaching was this supreme event which 'the prophets and Moses did say should come: that Christ should suffer, and that he should be the first that should rise from the dead.'[1]

It is not widely appreciated today that the resurrection of Christ is predicted in the books of Moses (the first five books of the Bible) as well as in the prophets, yet Paul showed that all the events of Christ's life were foretold in these books. In the last chapter of *Acts* Paul is viewed as a prisoner in his hired house, receiving Jewish leaders and

---

1 *Acts 26.22-23*

'persuading them concerning Jesus, both out of the law of Moses, and out of the prophets, from morning till evening.'[2] The narrative suggests that the Old Testament speaks *often* of the resurrection, the references being numerous enough for Paul to employ them at great length in convincing those doubting Jewish leaders.

The risen Saviour had previously taught the disciples along the same lines, saying, 'These are the words which I spake unto you, while I was yet with you, that all things must be fulfilled, which were written in the law of Moses, and in the prophets, and in the psalms, concerning me ... Thus it is written, and thus it behoved Christ to suffer, and to rise from the dead the third day.'[3]

This chapter will provide an opportunity to review some remarkable predictions in the Old Testament, and also to demonstrate that the Bible is not a disjointed collection of books, but a harmonious whole, Christ being the central theme throughout. A number of the prophecies mentioned here speak of the future resurrection of all believers, and some refer specifically to Christ's resurrection.

The First Resurrection Prediction

The first reference implying a resurrection of Christ comes in the promise of a Saviour made in *Genesis 3.15*, where God says to the serpent in the Garden of Eden: 'And I will put enmity between thee and the woman, and between thy seed and her seed; it shall bruise thy head, and thou shalt bruise his heel.' This is a fairly clear announcement of how Eve will have a glorious descendant who will counter the work of Satan to bring down the human race. In the process, this coming deliverer will be wounded and scarred, but this will not prove *permanently* fatal. The coming seed of the woman may be laid low for a time, but he will continue and be victorious. This very first reference to the coming of a Messiah, given at the very beginning of

---

2   *Acts 28.23*
3   *Luke 24.44-46*

Bible history, speaks of a *surviving, living* Saviour (later promises of a Saviour would speak more explicitly of his literal death as well as his survival).

We should be aware that throughout the Old Testament there are two great families of Scripture texts: those that speak of a coming Saviour who will die, and those that speak of that same Saviour triumphing and reigning. In the *Psalms*, for example, there are both *suffering* Messianic psalms, and *reigning* Messianic psalms. In *Isaiah*, there are similarly the *suffering servant* prophecies, and the *reigning king* references. These were not contradictory and confusing to readers in Bible times, because believing minds realised that the suffering and dying Saviour would also be the everlasting King. A resurrection was presumed and believed in. The possibility of confusion was not an issue. If Messiah died, plainly Messiah would rise again.

Prophecies in Historic Events

Before we look at more concrete prophecies, there were many hints or illustrations of the work of the coming deliverer written into the early history of the Jewish people, and deeply etched on their culture. One great theme running through the events of *Genesis* is that triumph and salvation arise from apparent defeat and death. Accordingly, Abraham left the safety and security of civilised Ur, proceeding into primitive and unknown regions, in order to reach a promised land which God would give to his descendants. Similarly, he and Sarah died in reproductive terms before a promised seed arose.[4] Isaac, by the command of the Lord, was to be offered up in sacrifice and symbolically raised from the 'dead' for the future life of the family of promise.[5]

Jacob returned to his father's house through a deep valley of anguish, facing certain death at the hand of Esau with 400 armed

---

4   *Hebrews 11.12*
5   *Hebrews 11.19*

men, and wrestling in prayer with the Angel of the Lord at Peniel. Only after humiliation was his life preserved. Only then, bearing the scar of his ordeal, did the sun rise upon him, and he 'passed over Penuel' to return home. Later, Joseph was left for dead in a pit, then sold into captivity to become the eventual saviour of his family. He was also arrested and humiliated, in order to gain the highest power.

Throughout the record of *Genesis*, famine leads to deliverance, and hardship leads to life. By these events God prepared the minds of Old Testament believers to understand that deliverance would come through a suffering deliverer, and resurrection life would follow apparent defeat and death. Their history and their culture told them that as a nation they would bring forth the Messiah, and that his suffering and subsequent victory were illustrated in historic types.

The Picture at Horeb

The resurrection of Christ is pictured by implication in the appearance of the Angel of the Lord to Moses as he approached Horeb while a shepherd in that region. The Lord appeared in a 'flame of fire out of the midst of a bush',[6] and Moses was startled by the remarkable resistance of that bush to the searing flame.[7] The sight of branches surviving the flames impressed upon the mind of Moses the *invincibility* of God, and the indestructibility of Messiah. In due course Moses would be told by God to inaugurate sacrifices that would illustrate the great future sacrifice of an atoning Saviour, but Moses would never forget that God's invincibility would also require his resurrection.

---

6   *Exodus 3.2*
7   Matthew Poole affirms the divinity of this angel, identifying him as – 'The Angel of the Lord; not a created angel, but the Angel of the Covenant, Jesus Christ, who then and ever was God, and was to be man, and to be sent into the world in our flesh, as a messenger from God. And these temporary apparitions of his were presages or forerunners of his more solemn mission and coming.'

The resurrection of believers in general at the end of the world is promised in the dramatic words that the Lord spoke to Moses at the burning bush, for he said, 'I am the God of thy father, the God of Abraham, the God of Isaac, and the God of Jacob.'[8] These patriarchs were all dead, but God declared that he was still their God at that very moment, for they were alive in his presence.

God's words only indicated that their *souls* were alive, but they include the assurance of a *bodily* resurrection to come for the following reason. The patriarchs had been specifically promised an innumerable offspring who would occupy a literal, physical land.[9] Abraham was also told he would receive this physical land for an everlasting possession.[10] He and his spiritual descendants would walk eternally on a beautiful and glorious Earth. Therefore the fact that the patriarchs were alive in their souls, and in the presence of God, gave assurance that God would one day keep his promise that they would have a *physical* earthly inheritance. It would have become obvious to Moses from God's words that they were reserved in Heaven for a future resurrection when a new, glorified Earth would become the eternal promised land for God's people.

We are told in *Hebrews 11* that this was exactly what the patriarchs themselves expected – a future fulfilment of the promises.

'By faith Abraham, when he was called to go out into a place which he should after receive for an inheritance, obeyed; and he went out, not knowing whither he went ... dwelling in tabernacles with Isaac and Jacob, the heirs with him of the same promise: for he looked for a city which hath foundations, whose builder and maker is God ... These all died in faith, not having received the promises, but having seen them afar off, and were persuaded of them, and embraced them, and confessed that they were strangers and pilgrims on the earth. For they that say such things declare plainly that they seek a country. And truly, if they had been mindful of that country from whence they came out, they might have had opportunity to have returned. But

8   *Exodus 3.6*
9   *Genesis 13.15*
10 *Genesis 17.8*

now they desire a better country, that is, an heavenly: wherefore God is not ashamed to be called their God: for he hath prepared for them a city' *(Hebrews 11.8-10, 13-16).*

The Lord Jesus Christ plainly stated that the words of God to Moses were all about the resurrection:–

'But as touching the resurrection[11] of the dead, have ye not read that which was spoken unto you by God, saying, I am the God of Abraham, and the God of Isaac, and the God of Jacob? God is not the God of the dead, but of the living' *(Matthew 22.31-32).*

The resurrection of Christ is therefore *pictured* in the appearance of the Lord to Moses at Horeb, while the resurrection of all believers is confirmed as a coming reality in God's assurance that the patriarchs were alive in glory. The promise of their bodily occupation of a literal land was still clearly in force.

Job's Revelation

Not long after the time of Abraham, suffering Job longed for death and extinction, but God gave him a view of a personal future resurrection when he would see *in bodily form* the Saviour who would redeem him.

'Oh that my words were now written! oh that they were printed in a book! That they were graven with an iron pen and lead in the rock for ever! For I know that my redeemer liveth, and that he shall stand at the latter day upon the earth: and though after my skin worms destroy this body, yet in my flesh shall I see God: whom I shall see for myself, and mine eyes shall behold, and not another; though my reins be consumed within me' *(Job 19.23-27).*

The truth of a future life *in the body,* even after his present body had rotted in the grave, was deeply impressed upon Job's mind. In the future he would see with physical eyes the God who would redeem him. Job had received an earlier assurance of a future life in chapter

---

11 The Greek word used by the Lord for resurrection refers to bodily resurrection, meaning – standing up.

14.14-15, but now he is further assured that it will be a *bodily* future life. This text does not refer to the resurrection of Christ, but it is very definite about the resurrection of people who believe in God as Job did.

Resurrection Prophecies in the Psalms

We have already observed that Christ, in one of his post-resurrection appearances, told the disciples that his resurrection was prefigured not only in the books of Moses, but also in the prophets and the *Psalms*, and this brings us to look at a number of significant passages.

It is worth mentioning first that the *Psalms* have many hints of the resurrection of believers generally. We have only to think of the numerous times David refers to infallible physical deliverances, vindications and prosperity that *all* God's people *will* experience, to realise he is speaking about a bodily future in an eternal paradise. It simply is not true that all believers are always saved from injury, hunger and oppression while in this life, and David as a king and military defender knew that very well. If he is thought to be describing believers in this present life, then he speaks as the most naive man on Earth, which he plainly was not. He obviously speaks of a future physical realm which God's people will enjoy for ever. In short, he uses resurrection language, and his numerous triumphalistic passages are prophecies of resurrection.

Resurrection Anticipated in Psalm 8

A very direct prophecy of Christ's resurrection shines out of *Psalm 8*, where David (speaking as a prophet) asks, 'What is man, that thou art mindful of him? and the son of man, that thou visitest him?'

This psalm is not merely an observation that God has elevated human beings above all other creatures on the Earth, but David here speaks of God coming to visit man in person. This was very beautifully asserted by J. J. Stewart Perowne in his great work on the

Psalms. He wrote: 'As the poet gazes on into the liquid depths of that starry sky there comes upon him with overwhelming force the sense of his own insignificance. This is the first feeling, but it is immediately swallowed up in another – the consciousness of the seed-royal, of the Second Adam, of highest lineage and dignity, crowned and sceptred as a king.'

David's words are certainly about a visitor far higher than ordinary men and women, who would ultimately be crowned to reign over all, and this is how the psalm is interpreted in the New Testament, where it is applied to the Saviour in *1 Corinthians 15.27*, and in *Hebrews 2.6-10*.

David sees a divine visitor who would stoop to human level and be made 'a little lower than the angels' (verse 5) in order to destroy God's enemies (verse 2), and then be 'crowned . . . with glory and honour' (verse 5) to have lordship over everything (verses 5-8). In its sweep the psalm covers the incarnation, the atoning work of Christ, and the resurrection.

Resurrection Stated in Psalm 16

Psalm 16, another prophetic utterance of David, speaks in an even more direct way of the coming Saviour's death and resurrection. The psalmist says: 'I have set the Lord always before me: because he is at my right hand, I shall not be moved. Therefore my heart is glad, and my glory rejoiceth: my flesh also shall rest in hope. For thou wilt not leave my soul in hell; neither wilt thou suffer thine Holy One to see corruption' (verses 8-10).

In his personal meditation David sets before him the certainty of Messiah's coming, and his saving, caring power. Then, as the king reflects on the glorious truth that he will live beyond death, it is revealed to him that Messiah will be the first to defy the grave, and he exclaims, 'Neither wilt thou suffer thine Holy One to see corruption' (verse 10). The King James translators have rightly used capital letters for 'Holy One' indicating that David refers here to Messiah and not to himself. In the first half of his statement he refers to himself, and in the second, to Christ. Here are verses 9 and 10 set out to reflect this vital distinction:–

> 'Therefore my heart is glad, and my glory rejoiceth: my flesh also shall rest in hope. For thou wilt not leave my soul in hell . . .
>
> 'Neither wilt thou suffer thine Holy One to see corruption.'

The apostles Peter and Paul both quote this psalm as a prophecy of Christ's resurrection.[12]

Death to Life in Psalm 22

In *Psalm 22*, a notable Messianic psalm, David is inspired to speak of the Saviour as though he is speaking of himself. But we are immediately aware that this is prophetic language because it describes a suffering far beyond anything ever endured by David or any other person apart from Christ. Furthermore, towards the end David switches tense to speak directly about Messiah's work and status.

The psalmist begins: 'My God, my God, why hast thou forsaken me?' then describes the terrible sufferings of Calvary in language unparalleled in all the scope of sacred Scripture. But Christ's agonies and torments are not the end. The language of death is not the conclusion of the prophecy, for the sufferer says – 'I will declare thy name unto my brethren' (verse 22). The language of the psalm becomes triumphant, speaking of the achievements of the sufferer's afflictions, and how people who seek the Lord will be benefited and live for ever. A future seed will glorify him, and all the earth (the Gentiles) will turn to him and worship him. This sufferer, clearly the Messiah, will take the kingdom, and govern over all, and his servants will proclaim the message of salvation to a people yet to be born.

How could anyone fail to see the atonement and the resurrection in this psalm? Humiliation and death, immediately followed by victorious kingship, must indicate resurrection. Without the suffering

---

12 *Acts 2.22-32; Acts 13.35-37*

Saviour rising from the dead this psalm would be a pathetic case of total self-contradiction.

Christ's Entry into Heaven in Psalm 24

Psalm 24 is yet another psalm of David picturing the resurrection of Christ in the typical language of Old Testament prophecy. The Tabernacle's holy of holies is used to describe the eternal dwelling-place of God, and the question is posed – Who shall ascend into it and stand in the holy place? This is more than, 'Who will go to Heaven?' The problem is that no one deserves to go to Heaven, and so the real question is – 'Who will be our representative and earn Heaven for us all?' The answer of the psalm is that Messiah alone can do this.

In those days, only the high priest, who would first wash to be made ceremonially pure, would enter the holy place. But David looks beyond him and ahead to the Saviour, who offered up his perfect life and entered Heaven for his people. The entry of the high priest into the holy of holies was a pictorial prophecy of the day when the victorious, conquering Saviour would cause the everlasting doors of Heaven to yield before him.

David's description of this event picks up the features of Solomon's Temple.[13] This incorporated suspended golden chain-gates in addition to double doors of fir, barring the way to the holy of holies. Through those doors went the high priest alone, and only once each year, wearing on his breast the names of the tribes. This annual entry prefigured the work of Christ who, having made a perfect offering for his people, would rise again and ascend on high; in the well-known words of Cecil Frances Alexander –

> The golden gates are lifted up,
> The doors are opened wide;
> The King of Glory is gone up
> Unto his Father's side.

13 Although David wrote in advance of the Temple, he had the plans.

Did the Jews in Old Testament times grasp that the action of the high priest was a prophetic picture of how the coming Messiah would enter into Heaven? They certainly did, or should have done, and *Hebrews 9.7-8* assures us of this, saying: 'But into the second *[the holy of holies]* went the high priest alone once every year, not without blood, which he offered for himself, and for the errors of the people: THE HOLY GHOST THIS SIGNIFYING, that the way into the holiest of all was not yet made manifest, while as the first tabernacle was yet standing.'

The Holy Spirit signified or showed the people in the days of the Tabernacle that the coming Messiah would deal with sin, and then enter Heaven as a victorious king. 'Who is this King of glory?' asks the psalmist, and the answer is not the high priest but 'the Lord of hosts'. Charles Wesley expands the psalm perfectly –

> 'Who is the King of Glory, who?'
> The Lord who all his foes o'ercame;
> The world, sin, death, and hell o'erthrew,
> And Jesus is the Conqueror's name.

> 'Who is the King of Glory, who?'
> The Lord of glorious power possessed,
> The King of saints and angels too:
> God over all, for ever blessed!

The Victorious Resurrection of Psalm 68

Psalm 68 focuses specifically on the risen Saviour in a magnificent song of resurrection and ascension (which is how Paul explains it in *Ephesians 4*).[14] David pictures the Lord leading his people, liberated from Egypt, through the wilderness and into Canaan, but it is obvious that the narrative is deployed as a prophecy about the future

---

14 'Wherefore he saith, When he ascended up on high, he led captivity captive, and gave gifts unto men. (Now that he ascended, what is it but that he also descended first into the lower parts of the earth? He that descended is the same also that ascended up far above all heavens, that he might fill all things)' *(Ephesians 4.8-10)*.

Messiah. The language is far too extravagant and spectacular to be intended as history. The words look forward to the Messiah – who 'rideth upon the heavens', and David says of him, 'Thou hast ascended on high, thou hast led captivity captive ... that the Lord God might dwell among them' (verse 18). Paul later asked – How could he ascend on high without first descending?

To the spiritually-minded Jew, David's words referred to the Messiah who would descend to Earth, engage in fierce battle, take the spoils of war and rise again to Heaven, so that people may dwell with God. David looks ahead and sees the descent and rescuing work of Christ, followed by his ascension.

Can we be sure that Jews in Old Testament times would have grasped the significance of these prophecies? The answer is, that earnest believers certainly did identify and value Messianic psalms. They studied such prophecies with the expectation of a coming Messiah firmly in their hearts as carefully as Christians do today.

Isaiah's Resurrection Prediction

One of the best Old Testament passages about the resurrection of Christ is *Isaiah 53*, a *suffering servant* prophecy. Not only is it gloriously clear and vivid in its explanation of Calvary, but it is also very strident in its announcement of a resurrection. Once again we ask – who could read the closing verses of this chapter without concluding that Messiah *must* rise again from his terrible death?

Isaiah 53.10 reads: 'Yet it pleased the Lord to bruise him; he hath put him to grief: when thou shalt make his soul an offering for sin, he shall see his seed, he shall prolong his days, and the pleasure of the Lord shall prosper in his hand.' Is it not obvious that he must rise in order to contemplate and enjoy his seed (his spiritual offspring), and certainly to prolong his days? After making a bodily sacrifice, he will live on!

Isaiah 53.11 includes the words: 'He shall see of the travail of his soul, and shall be satisfied.' It is the Saviour himself who views his sacrifice, which means that he is alive again to view the success of his atonement. We accept that these words carry a secondary meaning, also showing that even while hanging on the cross Christ could see in his mind's eye all those for whom he was dying. But the *primary* sense of these verses is that the dying Redeemer would live again to see his fruit, namely people saved down the centuries.

Isaiah 53.12 reads: 'Therefore will I divide him a portion with the great, and he shall divide the spoil with the strong.' This describes how the rewards and fruits of victory will rightly be given to a living and triumphant victor in battle. It is language which would be utterly inappropriate for one who still lay dead, never to be seen alive again. The resurrection language of this passage is immediately followed, not by a funeral dirge, but by a triumphant, stirring call to the church to rejoice, the very next chapter beginning – 'Sing, O barren, thou that didst not bear; break forth into singing.' Can we imagine such a clarion call to happiness and evangelism proceeding from the final, unalterable death of the Messiah?

Other Resurrection Passages

Other verses in the Old Testament tie a future life after death to a physical, bodily existence, although not specifically mentioning Messiah. In *Isaiah 25* a day of redemption is foretold, centred on a certain mountain, when God will 'swallow up death in victory', bless his people, and liberate the Earth from sin and rebellion.[15] In the following chapter the inspired prophet makes the momentous statement – 'Thy dead men shall live,'[16] followed by a call to the church to wait patiently until the time of indignation and judgement is past.

The well-known resurrection text in *Daniel 12.2* assured the Jews of old that people would one day be raised *bodily* in a general

---

15 *Isaiah 25.6-8*
16 *Isaiah 26.19*

resurrection, and face a final judgement: 'And many of them that sleep in the dust of the earth shall awake, some to everlasting life, and some to shame and everlasting contempt.'

Personal bodily resurrection is certainly announced in *Hosea 13.14* (at around 750 BC) where the prophet says: 'I will ransom them from the power of the grave; I will redeem them from death: O death, I will be thy plagues; O grave, I will be thy destruction.' These words are taken and applied to the believer's resurrection by Paul in *1 Corinthians 15.55*.

Once again we ask the question – Did the Jews of old grasp these prophecies of resurrection, and expect it? They certainly did, when they took their Scriptures seriously. In New Testament times the Sadducees denied that there would be a resurrection, but the Pharisees strongly disputed with them on this point.[17] Very many Jews believed in a resurrection.

The expectation of a Messiah (including his death and resurrection) was unquestionably deeply embedded in Jewish teaching as we see from the words of Martha of Bethany recorded in *John 11.21-27*. Her brother Lazarus had been dead in the grave four days when the Saviour arrived at Bethany in response to her call. Having arrived, the Lord uttered those great words – 'I am the resurrection, and the life,' and challenged Martha, asking: 'Believest thou this?' She replied, without any hesitation or difficulty, 'Yea, Lord: I believe that thou art the Christ, the Son of God, which should come into the world.' Martha knew what the Old Testament Scriptures taught, that Messiah would suffer and die, and yet would live for ever. She clearly knew and believed that Moses, the prophets and the *Psalms* provided the solution to that riddle, veiled though it was at times, that Messiah must rise from the dead. 'Of course,' said Martha, in effect, 'I realise that as the Christ, the Son of God, thou art the Lord of resurrection and life.'

---

17 *Acts 23.6-9*

When Christ came, the Jewish leaders in general had lost sight of the prophecies of a *suffering* Saviour who would subsequently defeat the grave, expecting instead a political deliverer, but they should not have done. The faithful, however, kept these things in their hearts.

Contrary to what is often thought by people not familiar with the Bible, there is not one God in the Old Testament and another in the New, the first being angry and remote, the second being kinder and nearer. There is no difference between the Testaments, everything in the New being prophesied and anticipated in the Old. Only resurrection prophecies have been mentioned in this chapter, but there are so many more, foretelling so much about Christ, his work, his church and his return, and all these fasten the two Testaments together in a message of love to lost mankind. Both speak of man's alienation from God and his redemption through the coming, the death and the resurrection of a Saviour. Both are about mercy, grace, salvation and eternal life, and hold out the same availability of pardon and new life to all who approach God in repentance and faith.

10
The Holy Trinity

Almighty God, to thee
  Be endless honours done,
The undivided Three,
  And the mysterious One.
Where reason fails, with all her powers,
There faith prevails and love adores.

THROUGHOUT THIS BOOK three divine persons have been repeatedly referred to, the Father, the Son, and the Holy Spirit, and each one assumes a role in the great plan of redemption. The Christian faith holds that there is only one true and sovereign God, but he is triune, meaning there are three persons in the Godhead. These three glorious persons are distinct and yet they are one, sharing the same spiritual essence, being in perfect agreement and harmony, and being equally eternal and omnipotent.[1] As an historic Confession of Faith puts it:

'In this Divine and infinite Being there are three subsistences,

---

1   *1 John 5.7; 2 Corinthians 13.14*

the Father, the Word or Son, and the Holy Spirit, of one substance, power, and eternity, each having the whole Divine essence, yet the essence undivided . . . which doctrine of the Trinity is the foundation of all our communion with God.'[2]

This doctrine is taught in both the Old and the New Testaments, clearly enough in the Old, and with blazing clarity in the New. The few Bible references shown in these pages to validate statements represent many more, and numerous great studies of the Trinity have been written listing them all.

In the first book of the Bible, God introduces himself using plural pronouns, showing that there are several members of the Godhead.[3] In Old Testament prophecy three divine persons are all mentioned in a single sentence – the Lord's servant (the divine Messiah), then the Lord God as a distinct person (clearly the Father), and the Spirit, again as a distinct person. There are two verses like this in *Isaiah*.[4] Clear references to the relationship between the Father and the Son are also found.[5]

The passages recording theophanies in the Old Testament (appearances of God in the form of a man) describe the person who appears as an angel (a messenger) who is shown to be God, and yet who is sent from God, very obviously showing two of the members of the Trinity.[6] And Christ is mentioned several times in prophecy as being distinct from God, and yet God himself.[7]

The Holy Spirit is also mentioned as one who is sent from God, yet who possesses his own divine power. References to the Holy Spirit

---

2   Chapter 2 and Section 3 of both the *Westminster Confession of Faith*, 1646, and *Baptist Confession of Faith* of 1689.

3   *Genesis 1.26; 11.7*

4   *Isaiah 48.16; 61.1*

5   *Psalm 45.6-7; Daniel 7.13-14*

6   *Genesis 31.11-13; Exodus 3.2-6; Exodus 23.23; Exodus 32.34; Joshua 5.13-15; Judges 6.11-24; Judges 13.1-25* (there are more theophanies, but only references that show specifically that the divine person who appears is the messenger of the Lord are listed).

7   Eg: *Isaiah 7.14; Isaiah 9.6-7*

do not merely describe how God exercises his power, but show him to be a distinct, separate person of the Godhead.[8] Also, we read of how God sends his Holy Spirit.[9]

Believers in Old Testament times knew well that a Messiah would come from God who would himself be a divine person, and that a wonderful Holy Spirit also possessing divine power did great things on God's behalf. By the time Christ came, his own divinity (and that of the Spirit) presented no novelty to the first disciples, because the three persons of the Godhead were already known from the Old Testament. At Pentecost there was no consternation whatsoever among those early believers, and no shrinking back from the forthright teaching of God as triune.

Throughout the New Testament the Lord Jesus Christ is very obviously God the eternal Son. It is made clear that he did not become divine as a reward for Calvary, but had always from eternity been equal with the Father. (This is so important that a number of texts are provided to confirm this point.[10])

The words of the prophet Daniel are extremely important in understanding how Christ described himself, because the prophet spoke about a divine person called 'the Son of man' who would be given an earthly kingdom. This was the term adopted by the Lord to describe himself. Daniel's words read:–

'I saw in the night visions, and, behold, one like the Son of man came with the clouds of heaven, and came to the Ancient of days, and they brought him near before him. And there was given him dominion, and glory, and a kingdom, that all people, nations, and languages, should serve him: his dominion is an everlasting dominion, which shall not pass away, and his kingdom that which shall not be destroyed.'[11]

---

8   Eg: *Isaiah 48.16*
9   *Joel 2.28-32*
10 *Micah 5.2; John 1.1-4; John 8.56-58; John 17.5, 24, 25; Romans 9.5;
    Philippians 2.5-7; Colossians 1.15-17*
11 *Daniel 7.13-14*

The Lord Jesus Christ repeatedly spoke of himself as the Son of man, and his Jewish hearers, being aware that this was Daniel's term for a divine person, realised that he was calling himself God.[12] Daniel saw the 'Ancient of days' give the Son of man total and eternal dominion. (The Lord's assumption of this divine title is recorded so many times, and is so significant, that many texts are listed below, and this does not exhaust the number.[12])

The Lord himself spoke often of his relationship with the Father.[13] He was authenticated and owned by the Father's voice from Heaven at his baptism, when the Holy Spirit also joined with him for his ministry on Earth.[14]

All three members of the Trinity are mentioned by Matthew when he describes Christ giving the great commission to his disciples: 'Go ye therefore, and teach all nations, baptizing them in the name of the Father, and of the Son, and of the Holy Ghost.'[15]

Jesus Christ is presented throughout the New Testament as possessing all the attributes of God, Paul saying: 'For in him dwelleth all the fulness of the Godhead bodily,'[16] and also: 'In whom are hid all the treasures of wisdom and knowledge.'[17]

The Holy Spirit came most prominently with all his divine power on the Day of Pentecost, to perform the work of the risen Saviour in souls and in true churches. It is he who regenerates hearts, illuminates minds, draws to Christ, and brings about the transformation of conversion.[18]

The biblical doctrine of the Trinity is a foundation of salvation because it provides for the coming of a Saviour for lost mankind.

---

12 Eg: *Matthew 16.13; Matthew 19.28; Mark 8.31, 38; Luke 6.22; Luke 9.22, 26; Luke 12.8; Luke 22.48; John 3.13; John 5.27*
13 Eg: *Matthew 11.27; John 5.17-38*
14 *Matthew 3.16-17*
15 *Matthew 28.19*
16 *Colossians 2.9*
17 *Colossians 2.3*
18 *Acts 2; John 15.26; Galatians 4.6*

The Father acts for the whole Godhead, while the Son enters human flesh to take the place of sinners. The Father pours out his justice and punishment upon the Son, who bears it away for sinners. This is traditionally illustrated in Christian theology as the Father promising to give the Son a people for his eternal possession if the Son will go to Earth and die to redeem them. The Son has now done just this, and so the Holy Spirit, for his part, will work in the hearts of all who will be saved, until the kingdom of Christ is complete.

Several passages of Scripture are erroneously thought of by cults as limiting the power of Christ, and making him less than divine. For example, Christ said that the Son could do nothing of himself[19] and that the Father was greater than himself.[20] But such passages do not take away Christ's divine power, as he himself explained. The Lord had come to put himself in the place of human beings, and to be subject to the law of God, so that he would live a perfectly obedient life on behalf of those he would save. His life on Earth was the time of his voluntary humiliation as a representative man, and so he appears to be subordinate to the Father, which he never had been in eternity past, nor would be in the eternal future. When he pointed out that he did nothing except what the Father directed, he was saying that he and the Father were in perfect harmony, not that he was inferior, and therefore not God.

Sometimes the question is asked – how could Christ be God when he did not know everything? This query comes from the occasion when the Lord spoke about the end of the world, adding, 'But of that day and that hour knoweth no man, no, not the angels which are in heaven, neither the Son, but the Father.'[21]

Some people have tried to solve the problem of these puzzling words by saying that Christ knew the time of the end in his *divine*

---

19 *John 5.19, 30*
20 *John 14.28*
21 *Mark 13.32*

nature but not in his *human* nature. However, Christ's two natures, though distinct, were wholly blended, so that he was truly God and man together. It is not possible that part of him knew something and another part did not. He knew all things.[22]

The Lord meant that he could not have known about the time of the end by virtue of his human nature and intelligence, because it was something that could never be calculated or guessed by a created being, not even by angels. But he did know the time when the world would end, because he was also divine. He had virtually told the disciples that he knew all about these things in the long preceding statement.[23] Then he declared that he could not have known these things had he only been a man.

The Lord's mysterious words should never be interpreted so as to overthrow the overwhelming number of clear statements in the New Testament that he was the divine Messiah.

The Lord Jesus Christ whom Christian believers know and love is the pre-existing second person of the Trinity,[24] the creator of all things,[25] the author of the Bible,[26] the light of the world,[27] the giver of spiritual life to needy souls,[28] the Son of God who entered the world to secure salvation,[29] and the Saviour who bids people to come to him,[30] forgiving their sins,[31] and answering their prayers.[32] He will come again in power and glory[33] to be the final judge,[34] and

---

22 *Matthew 11.27; John 5.20*
23 *Mark 13.24-31*
24 *John 8.56-58,* and footnote 10 references on page 115
25 *John 1.3, 10*
26 *John 1.1*
27 *John 8.12*
28 *John 5.21*
29 *Matthew 20.28; John 3.16*
30 *Matthew 11.28*
31 *Matthew 9.6*
32 *John 14.13*
33 *Matthew 16.27; 1 Corinthians 1.7*
34 *John 5.27; 2 Timothy 4.8*

to be the King of his ransomed people in eternal glory.[35]

'Christ is all!' exclaimed the apostle Paul. May he be Lord and God of all who read these pages, and may the same apostle's prayer be answered:–

'For this cause I bow my knees unto the Father of our Lord Jesus Christ, of whom the whole family in heaven and earth is named, that he would grant you, according to the riches of his glory, to be strengthened with might by his Spirit in the inner man; that Christ may dwell in your hearts by faith; that ye, being rooted and grounded in love, may be able to comprehend with all saints what is the breadth, and length, and depth, and height; and to know the love of Christ, which passeth knowledge, that ye might be filled with all the fulness of God. Now unto him that is able to do exceeding abundantly above all that we ask or think, according to the power that worketh in us, unto him be glory in the church by Christ Jesus throughout all ages, world without end. Amen' *(Ephesians 3.14-21).*

35 *James 2.1, 5*

Faith, Doubts, Trials and Assurance
139 pages, paperback, ISBN 1 870855 50 7

Ongoing faith is essential for answered prayer, effective service, spiritual stability and real communion with God. In this book many questions are answered about faith, such as –

How may we assess the state of our faith? How can faith be strengthened? What are the most dangerous doubts? How should difficult doubts be handled? What is the biblical attitude to trials? How can we tell if troubles are intended to chastise or to refine? What can be done to obtain assurance? What are the sources of assurance? Can a believer commit the unpardonable sin? Exactly how is the Lord's presence felt?

Dr Masters provides answers, with much pastoral advice, drawing on Scripture throughout.

The Baptist Confession of Faith of 1689
Updated with notes by Peter Masters
53 pages, paperback, ISBN 1 870855 24 8

C. H. Spurgeon said of this great Confession – 'Here the youngest members of our church will have a body of Truth in small compass, and by means of the scriptural proofs, will be able to give a reason of the hope that is in them.'

This brilliant summary of doctrine (in the same family as the Westminster Confession), with its invaluable proof texts, is here gently modernised in punctuation, with archaic words replaced. Explanations of difficult phrases have been added in italic brackets. A brief history of the Confession, with an index, is included.

Heritage of Evidence

127 pages, illustrated, paperback, ISBN 1 870855 39 6

In today's atheistic climate most people have no idea how much powerful evidence exists for the literal accuracy and authenticity of the biblical record. The British Museum holds a huge number of major discoveries that provide direct corroboration and background confirmation for an immense sweep of Bible history. This survey of Bible-authenticating exhibits has been designed as a guide for visitors, and also to give pleasure and interest to readers unable to tour the galleries. It will also be most suitable for people who need to see the accuracy and inspiration of the Bible.

The 'tour' followed here started life over forty years ago and has been used by many thousands of people including youth and student groups.

Almost every item viewed on the tour receives a full colour photograph. Room plans are provided for every gallery visited showing the precise location of artefacts, and time-charts relate the items to contemporary kings and prophets. The book is enriched by pictures and descriptions of famous 'proofs' in other museums.

Men of Purpose

157 pages, illustrated, paperback, ISBN 1 870855 41 8

This book brings into one illustrated volume eleven great lives, all with an experience of personal conversion to God. Composer Mendelssohn, food industrialist Henry Heinz, novelist Daniel Defoe, and some of the most celebrated scientists of all time, are among the examples of leading people whose lives were changed by a sight of real Christianity. Also very suitable as a gift to unconverted friends, and to enrich sermons and Bible class messages.

Not Like Any Other Book
161 pages, paperback, ISBN 1 870855 43 4

Faulty Bible interpretation lies at the root of every major mistake and 'ism' assailing churches today, and countless Christians are asking for the old, traditional and proven way of handling the Bible to be spelled out plainly.

A new approach to interpretation has also gripped many evangelical seminaries and Bible colleges, an approach based on the ideas of unbelieving critics, stripping the Bible of God's message, and leaving pastors impoverished in their preaching.

This book reveals what is happening, providing many brief examples of right and wrong interpretation. The author shows that the Bible includes its own rules of interpretation, and every believer should know what these are.

Physicians of Souls
The Gospel Ministry
285 pages, paperback, ISBN 1 870855 34 5

'Compelling, convicting, persuasive preaching, revealing God's mercy and redemption to dying souls, is seldom heard today. The noblest art ever granted to our fallen human race has almost disappeared.'

Even where the free offer of the Gospel is treasured in principle, regular evangelistic preaching has become a rarity, contends the author. These pages tackle the inhibitions, theological and practical, and provide powerful encouragement for physicians of souls to preach the Gospel. A vital anatomy or order of conversion is supplied with advice for counselling seekers.

The author shows how passages for evangelistic persuasion may be selected and prepared. He also challenges modern church growth techniques, showing the superiority of direct proclamation. These and other key topics make up a complete guide to soul-winning.

God's Rules for Holiness
Unlocking the Ten Commandments
139 pages, paperback, ISBN 1 870855 37 X

Taken at face value the Ten Commandments are binding on all people, and will guard the way to Heaven, so that evil will never spoil its glory and purity. But the Commandments are far greater than their surface meaning, as this book shows.

They challenge us as Christians on a still wider range of sinful deeds and attitudes. They provide positive virtues as goals. And they give immense help for staying close to the Lord in our walk and worship.

The Commandments are vital for godly living and for greater blessing, but we need to enter into the panoramic view they provide for the standards and goals for redeemed people.

Worship in the Melting Pot
148 pages, paperback, ISBN 1 870855 33 7

'Worship is truly in the melting pot,' says the author. 'A new style of praise has swept into evangelical life shaking to the foundations traditional concepts and attitudes.' How should we react? Is it all just a matter of taste and age? Will churches be helped, or changed beyond recognition?

This book presents four essential principles which Jesus Christ laid down for worship, and by which every new idea must be judged.

Here also is a fascinating view of how they worshipped in Bible times, including their rules for the use of instruments, and the question is answered – What does the Bible teach about the content and order of a service of worship today?

Joshua's Conquest
Was it Moral? What does it say to us today?
119 pages, paperback, ISBN 1 870855 46 9

Rooted and grounded in love for the Lord, Joshua was utterly faithful, wonderfully stable, and scrupulously obedient. The book of the Bible that bears his name is a magnificent anthology of events to challenge and inspire God's children in every age.

This is a book for reading, rather than a commentary. Its aim is to bring out the spiritual message of *Joshua* for today, and also to explain some of the 'problem' portions and passages which evoke questions on, for example, the morality of so much killing, and whether God was responsible for hardening the hearts of the Canaanites. In *Joshua* we find the holiness and mercy of God fully displayed, and numerous encouragements for the spiritual life.

The Mutual Love of Christ and His People
An explanation of the *Song of Solomon* for personal devotions and Bible study groups
115 pages, paperback, ISBN 1 870855 40 X

The courtship of the *Song of Solomon* provides fascinating scenes and events designed to show the love of Christ for His redeemed people, and theirs for Him. Here, also, are lessons for Christians when they become cold or backslidden, showing the way to recover Christ's presence in their lives.

Prophecies of Christ abound in the *Song*, together with views of the bride's destiny, as she prepares to cross the mountains into eternal glory, where the greatest wedding of all will take place.

This book begins with a brief overview of the reasons why the *Song* should be seen as allegorical – the viewpoint held through-out church history by the overwhelming majority of preachers and commentators. Then, in verse-by-verse mode, but designed for continuous devotional reading, the symbols are explained and applied.

Testimonies to the blessing obtained through this treatment of the *Song* have come from all over the world, from ministers and 'lay' people alike.

Missionary Triumph Over Slavery
William Knibb & Jamaican Emancipation
51 pages, illustrated, paperback, ISBN 1 870855 53 1

We are being told today that Christian missionaries of the past were tools of colonial oppression and destroyers of culture. The story of missionary William Knibb shows how wildly wrong this is. Persecuted by British rulers in Jamaica because he opposed settlers' abuses, he was pivotal in swinging British public opinion behind legislation to end colonial slavery. This is the true story of valiant missionary work covering the emancipation of slaves and the great Jamaican Awakening.

The Lord's Pattern for Prayer
118 pages, paperback, ISBN 1 870855 36 1

Subtitled – 'Studying the lessons and spiritual encouragements in the most famous of all prayers.' This volume is almost a manual on prayer, providing a real spur to the devotional life. The Lord's own plan and agenda for prayer – carefully amplified – takes us into the presence of the Father, to prove the privileges and power of God's promises to those who pray.

Chapters cover each petition in the Lord's Prayer. Here, too, are sections on remedies for problems in prayer, how to intercede for others, the reasons why God keeps us waiting for answers, and the nature of the prayer of faith.

Only One Baptism of the Holy Spirit
109 pages, paperback, ISBN 1 870855 17 5

The Healing Epidemic
227 pages, paperback, ISBN 1 870855 00 0

Steps for Guidance
184 pages, paperback, ISBN 1 870855 19 1

For other Wakeman titles please see: www.wakemantrust.org